FUNDAMENTALS OF PROCEDURE WRITING

Second Edition

FUNDAMENTALS OF PROCEDURE WRITING

Second Edition

Carolyn M. Zimmerman ■ John J. Campbell

GP PUBLISHING, INC.
Columbia, Maryland

GP Publishing, Inc.
5829 Banneker Road
Columbia, MD 21044

Library of Congress Cataloging-in-Publication Data
Zimmerman, Carolyn M., 1949-
Fundamentals of procedure writing / Carolyn M. Zimmerman and John J. Campbell.—2nd ed.
p. cm.
Bibliography: p.
Includes index.
ISBN 0-87683-942-1 :
1. Technical manuals. 2. Technical writing. I. Campbell, John J. (John Joseph), 1943—. II. Title.
T11.Z555 1988
808'0666021—dc19 88-16388
CIP

Printed and bound in the United States of America
94 93 92 91 90 89 88 5 4 3 2 1

Contents

Figures

Tables

1

Introduction

Effective written procedures and work instructions are critical to worker accuracy and efficiency in performing a task. A procedure's effectiveness depends essentially on two criteria: the accuracy of the information and the way in which the information is presented. A technically accurate procedure may not be usable or effective because the writer did not consider the factors—internal and external—that affect the procedure user's comprehension.

The purpose of this book is not only to make writers aware of these "human factors" so that they can apply writing principles that take these factors into account, but also to help writers write procedures more efficiently. Most people who write on the job have some kind of deadline or time restriction, and the techniques in this book are designed to streamline the procedure writing task to reduce the time required to produce a procedure and any anxiety connected with the writing task.

This text presents a process approach to developing effective procedures of all types, from a procedure on completing an expense report to a procedure on operating a turbine-generator. The logical steps of the writing process—plan, draft, and review—are applied to procedure writing, with a system of techniques for the writer at each step.

This text defines a procedure as a set of instructions that describes a task or process. Statements of policy or philosophy are sometimes misnamed "Corporate Procedures." This text discusses skills and techniques to develop true procedures, that is, instructions for a task or process, rather than descriptive statements of policy or philosophy.

1.1 CHAPTER OBJECTIVES

At the conclusion of this chapter, you should be able to:

1.1 List the three stages of the procedure development process.

1.2 State the roles and responsibilities of the writer, user, and reviewer in the procedure development process.

1.3 Name the elements of the communication cycle and discuss how each element affects procedure performance.

1.4 List the levels of comprehension and describe how each level is considered in procedure writing.

1.2 PROCESS OVERVIEW

Figure 1-1 shows a typical procedure writing process. The figure illustrates the stages of the process—plan, draft, and review—and the components of each stage. It also includes the user in the process (Blocks 13 and 14) because user feedback on problems in using the procedure is essential to making it workable.

1.3 RESPONSIBILITIES IN THE PROCESS: WRITER, REVIEWER, AND USER

Three people have a major part in producing an effective procedure: the writer, reviewer, and user. Their typical responsibilities are discussed below.

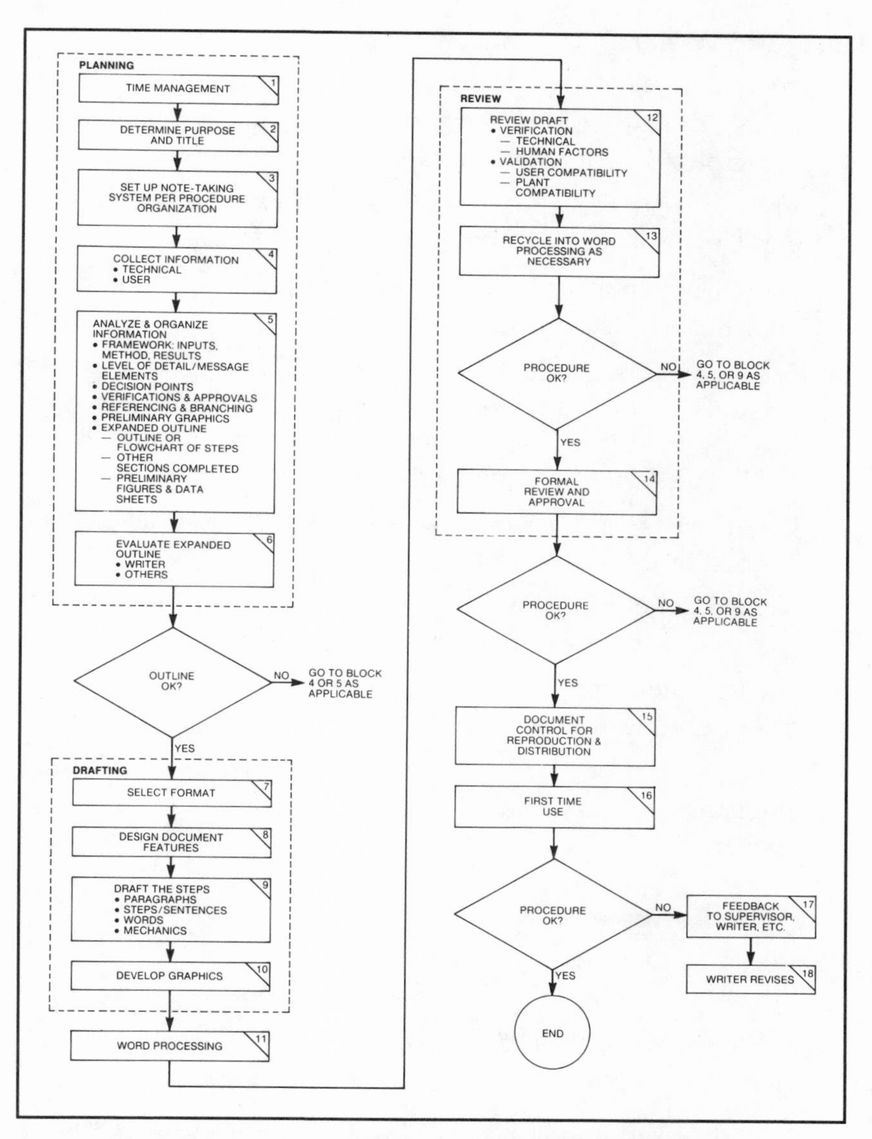

Figure 1-1. Typical Procedure Writing Process

1.3.1 The Writer

The procedure writer:

- Plans, drafts, and reviews the procedure using the principles described in this book
- Ensures that the procedure complies with applicable company policies and requirements
- Plans illustrations such as figures, tables, and forms, and coordinates their production
- Edits and proofreads the procedure draft and corrected versions after word processing or typing (If the company has a publications department, the writer coordinates editing and proofreading by the department staff.)
- Coordinates informal reviews of the procedure as described in this book
- Initiates the formal review and approval process as required by company policy
- Incorporates and resolves comments from procedure reviewers and users
- Reviews the procedure and revises it if necessary at regular intervals (annually, biennially, etc.) as required by company policy

1.3.2 The Reviewer

The procedure reviewer:

- Reviews the procedure informally at the writer's request using a review checklist as suggested by this book
- Returns specific review comments to the writer promptly
- If part of the formal review and approval process, uses a review checklist to ensure the procedure meets company policies and requirements for formal review

1.3.3 The User

The procedure user:

- Provides task information at the writer's request during the planning stage
- Informally reviews and comments on a procedure at the writer's request
- Notes problems while using a procedure, especially a new one
- Provides feedback to the writer on these problems

1.4 COMMUNICATING WITH THE WRITTEN WORD

Ideas are communicated through the language skills of writing, reading, listening, and speaking. Each person has a unique level of being able to communicate information using one or more of these skills. Communicating ideas through written procedures requires an interaction between the reader and the written document. Thus, a procedure's effectiveness depends as much on the skill of the reader as it does on the writing skills of the writer.

This interaction between the reader and the written procedure is often the root cause of procedure-related problems. Problems may occur because the written word is not the most efficient and effective method for communicating information. To evaluate the validity of this statement, consider a situation where you were able to verbally explain a concept or idea to someone clearly and concisely. The words and ideas flowed smoothly as you explained your concept to the other person. You watched the other person's verbal and nonverbal feedback to gauge the person's comprehension. You were able to communicate an idea successfully.

Now consider a task that required you to write about a concept or idea. If you were unable to develop a written product with the same speed, clarity, and conciseness as your verbal message, you have experienced the difficulty in conveying information through writing. This difficulty arose internally, that is, within such variables as your feelings about writing, writing speed, and your writing vocabulary versus your speaking vocabulary.

Additional difficulties can occur because each of your readers has a unique set of variables such as reading skills, background of knowledge in the idea you are communicating, and purpose or motivation for reading your product.

As a writer, you cannot use your verbal and nonverbal language skills to explain an idea. You cannot evaluate the other person's comprehension by observing and evaluating verbal and nonverbal feedback. The reader cannot hear your words and observe your nonverbal communication such as your attitude and conviction about the importance of your idea. Thus, the most effective means of communicating—face-to-face verbal—cannot be used. The language skills that tend to be least effective—writing and reading—become the main language skills used to communicate information through procedures. Moreover, written communication needs to be more precise than verbal because you don't get a second chance to explain if your reader doesn't understand what you have written.

Before developing or revising a procedure, you should understand the principal tenets of the communication process. You will then understand the reasons for the techniques suggested throughout the remainder of this text.

Without considering these communication factors, you may continue to focus on the technical aspects of the information and ignore the communication factors that will ultimately affect the usefulness of the procedure. Discussed here are the communication cycle and the three levels of reading comprehension and their effect on procedure development and use.

1.4.1 The Communication Cycle

The principles and practices recommended in this text are based on the elements in the communication cycle. The cycle as shown in Figure 1-2 has four elements: message, medium,

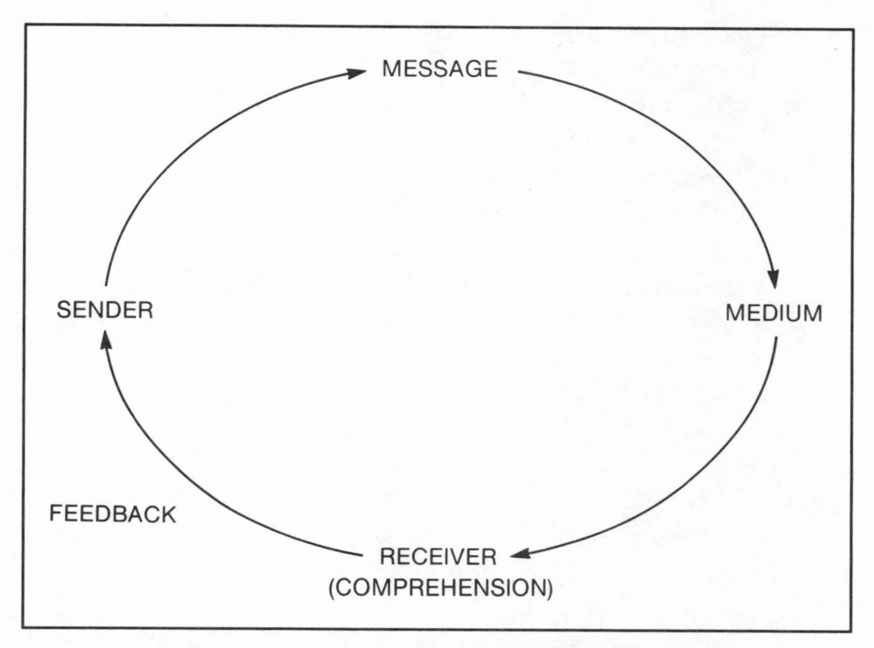

Figure 1-2. The Communication Cycle

receiver, and sender. The term "feedback" indicates the path followed by the receiver to indicate to the sender whether the message was comprehended.

Communication is the process of the interaction of these elements so that the message developed and presented by the sender is understood by the receiver. At any stage of the communication process the cycle can be interrupted, resulting in a lack of communication. Each element's relationship to the procedure writing process is explained below.

Message. The message developed by the procedure writer consists of all the information in the procedure. The "message" includes the types of information, such as the technical content that should be in a particular procedure, and the quantity of information, such as the appropriate level of detail for the intended users, and the sequence of that information, such as the logical organization of the tasks and steps in the procedure.

The writer must constantly consider the message as being developed from a global as well as a specific perspective. For example, since the message consists of all the information in the procedure, to achieve communication the user must understand all the information in the procedure and perform the steps as intended. From the specific perspective, the writer must consider all the contents in the procedure for global communication to occur. Thus, the writer must ensure that all sections of the procedure are written for the user to comprehend; all steps are clear, concise statements the user can implement; and all figures and data sheets available to the user help in achieving the purpose of the procedure.

The writer of a procedure must consider the global message as a series of specific messages developed to attain a specific purpose. Obviously, some global messages are easier to develop than others. A short procedure explaining how to complete a simple form requires less message analysis than a procedure that requires a great deal of information about a complex series of tasks.

Generally, the message is developed during the planning stage (Chapter 2), refined during the drafting stage (Chapter 3), and evaluated during the review stage of the writing process (Chapter 4).

Medium. The medium of the message refers to its "packaging." This packaging is crucial to the effectiveness of the procedure. Like the message, the medium must be considered on both global and specific levels. On the global level, the medium consists of the structure or sections the user expects to see. On the specific level, the medium includes format features as well as the writing style, language, and location of the information.

How the readability of the procedure affects its usefulness is discussed further in Chapter 2, and specifics on "packaging" a procedure are discussed in Chapter 3.

Sender. The procedure writer is the sender of the message. The procedure writer creates the message and packages the message in such a way that the user can read, understand, and perform the procedure as intended. The procedure writer must consider all the elements of the communication cycle while creating and packaging the message.

Many procedure comprehension problems arise because the procedure writer did not consider these elements when developing a procedure. Procedure writers must understand that the procedure is not being written for them. The procedure is written as a means of fostering standard methods of operations. Too many procedure writers concentrate on presenting only the technical facts, ignoring the communication elements that affect the usefulness of a procedure. An important point to remember throughout the procedure writing process is that having all the facts needed to perform a task does not mean that the task will be performed as intended. The procedure writer considers the needs of the user while organizing and packaging the technical facts.

Other personnel who review, comment on, or revise procedures also act as "senders." However, the writer has the ultimate responsibility, and it is the writer who is addressed throughout this book.

Receiver. The receiver ultimately judges the usefulness of the procedure by performance. For the most part, the main receiver of the message that the sender creates and packages is the user of the procedure. However, several other receivers read the procedure, including supervisors, peers, outside evaluators, and members of other departments that may be required to review your procedure. As mentioned above, these personnel are senders when they comment on or revise a procedure.

Far too often the receiver or user is not adequately considered in the procedure writing process. In fact, we have heard many times that members of a procedure development group never ask users to comment on a procedure until it has been through a formal approval process. Thus, the user is required to perform a procedure as written even though the user could have identified procedure-related problems much earlier in the process. In actuality, the burden falls on the user to suggest changes to the procedure, usually in a formal written request, after it has been approved and issued. Many times the users neither see other changes requested nor find out whether their suggestions were included (or why not).

The procedure writer must constantly write to satisfy the needs of the user. Specific techniques for user analysis are discussed in Chapter 2.

1.4.2 Levels of Comprehension

Comprehension of a procedure results when the user reads the procedure and performs the tasks as stated. Comprehension has three levels: literal, interpretive, and applied. These levels apply to both the writer and the user.

The Writer. The writer reads the literal technical facts (literal level). The writer then interprets how the facts are related, such as determining a specific sequence and decision points (interpretive level). The writer then writes the instructions for the user (applied level). The writer ensures that the user does *not* have to function at the interpretive level of comprehension by interpreting the relationships of ideas in advance.

The User. The user achieves the literal level of comprehension when he/she understands the facts presented in a procedure. All the technical facts related to performing the tasks in the procedure are considered to be at the literal level.

As stated above, the user should not have to operate at the interpretive level. The interpretive level operates when a relationship among literal facts is recognized. The most common types of relationships the writer identifies for the user are time order and cause and effect. When a user has to ask questions, he/she is trying to interpret the information. For example, the procedure calls for six steps to be performed. If the user must ask "Do these steps have to be performed in a certain sequence?," the user is seeking to make an interpretation that should have been made by the writer. Errors caused by requiring the user to interpret information include performing steps out of sequence because the writer did not specify the appropriate sequence, and equipment damage because the writer did not consider the cause and effect relationship between an action and the consequence of the action. The more interpretation required of the user, the longer the response time and the greater the probability of error.

When a user reads a procedure and performs the tasks as stated, the applied level is achieved. Thus, the user should be able to understand the procedure at the literal level, avoid having to interpret, and apply the information as stated.

Now that we understand some basic concepts of communication and comprehension, we are ready to enter the planning stage. Turn to Chapter 2.

2

Planning Stage

Many procedure writers, when given the assignment to develop a procedure, jump right into the first draft without planning the procedure. The result is often a disorganized product with significant omissions of content and a great deal of content that is not relevant or is at least only marginally useful to the procedure user. Devoting appropriate time to planning will shorten the drafting and review stages, so that the total time spent in procedure development is actually less than if the draft were begun with little or no planning. In business and industry, it seems that there is never enough time to plan a document carefully, but if the draft does not meet with management approval, there is always plenty of time to revise and rewrite, and rewrite again if necessary. Proper planning avoids numerous and massive rewrites at the end, because, as you will see in this chapter, the writer involves other personnel in the planning process, the same personnel who will in the end review and possibly request those rewrites after you have submitted your draft.

2.1 CHAPTER OBJECTIVES

At the conclusion of this chapter, you will be able to:

2.1 State a method of time management so that a procedure can be written efficiently and on time.

2.2 Name the first two products that must be developed before any other planning activities.

2.3 List the major steps in the planning process.

2.4 List types of technical information that can be used to develop a procedure.

2.5 List the three major categories of readability factors that affect the procedure user.

2.6 Describe a system for taking and organizing notes that puts information in the order needed to begin drafting the procedure.

2.7 List the message elements to consider and discuss how they relate to the level of detail to include in a procedure.

2.8 Describe types of verifications and approvals to consider in the planning stage.

2.9 Define referencing and branching and list some problems that they can cause in procedures.

2.10 Name and define the final product of the planning stage.

2.11 State the rationale for evaluating the final planning product.

2.2 TIME MANAGEMENT

Writers in many professions complain about the lack of time they are given to produce a document. In many situations this fact is true, but more often than not writers do not use available time efficiently. Writers who are the most vocal about lack of time are also guilty of procrastination and underestimating the time needed to write the document.

The following recommendations and techniques will help you more efficiently use the time you have to write a procedure. These recommendations are especially important if you have other responsibilities besides procedure writing.

2.2.1 Managing Your Time

Time management skills help prevent you from procrastinating or from falling prey to "writer's block." If you view procedure development as a series of schedules related to the writing process, you can become better organized and focus on the tasks needed to complete the procedure.

Of the three stages of procedure development—planning, drafting, and review—planning will require 40 to 60 percent of the total time you have to write the procedure. Committing this amount of time to planning means that the final planning product must be a nearly complete procedure. Such products as "rough drafts" and "preliminary drafts" are eliminated in this method.

As stated in the opening paragraphs to this chapter, sufficient time spent in planning reduces the time required for the other process stages. The drafting stage becomes a process of fine tuning the planning product to meet the guidelines discussed in Chapter 3. The review stage, both the review conducted by the writer and by others, is also reduced because the procedure will have fewer problems.

This approach to the procedure development process also holds true when you are tasked with revising a procedure. Many planning tasks will already have been accomplished by the original writer, so you can focus your time on those steps in the planning process that will help you complete the revision.

2.2.2 Developing Schedules

Generally, time can be controlled. You need to take control of your time by analyzing how you spend your writing time and developing time management goals and objectives. Goals and objectives are important simply because you are likely to put forth the effort to achieve them. Unless you have specific time goals and objectives, you are likely to postpone your writing.

Consider these techniques:

1. Analyze your schedule. Look at the time you have available between now and when the procedure is due. Identify the blocks of time you cannot use for writing, for example,

a weekly department meeting or a scheduled family vacation. Subtract these blocks of time from the total calendar time.

2. Estimate the time you will need to complete each stage of the writing process. Don't forget to allow for typing time and time to produce graphics.
3. Make up a schedule or time line for each process stage. For example, consider the time you have to complete planning, and estimate the time needed to perform each step in the planning stage. Refine your schedule as you complete each stage.
4. Make a daily writing schedule, estimating by blocks of hours the time needed to complete a task. Review the schedule at the end of each block to determine how well you kept to the schedule. Also, develop tomorrow's writing schedule, taking into account the time needed to complete today's task(s).

Remember that you are estimating the time needed, and these estimates will undoubtedly need some adjustment. If your estimates are off by 30 percent or more, determine which task took you more time and try to analyze why. Use this information to improve your estimating for the next writing assignment. After making up several schedules, you will have a better idea of how much time it actually takes you to complete a writing task, and your estimates will be closer to the actual time you need.

2.3 DETERMINING THE PURPOSE AND THE TITLE

You have received an assignment to write or revise a procedure. Your supervisor has given you the topic. Before you start planning your procedure's content, you need to be sure that you have a clear understanding of the objective the procedure should achieve. While this concept may seem obvious, we have reviewed many procedures in which the purpose statement did not match the procedure content. Also, a procedure may go beyond its stated purpose, or it may not completely fulfill it. Thus, it is essential at this point to be perfectly clear on the purpose of the procedure assigned to you. If you are not, you should ask your supervisor for clarification.

Your first written products are the purpose statement and the procedure title. Before you proceed further, write a brief but complete purpose statement. Begin with the word "To." Then, write a title. The title should be as brief as possible but specific enough to identify the major function to be achieved by the procedure and also to distinguish it from similar procedures. A good rule of thumb is a maximum of ten words, but this cannot always be met. Be sure that key words, such as the equipment name if any, are near the beginning of the title. Some companies have a computerized database of all procedures, and require that the first word of every technical procedure be the name of the equipment involved. This technique is handy for the procedure writer because he/she can obtain a list of all procedures dealing with a certain piece of equipment by performing a first word sort on the database.

2.4 PROCEDURE ORGANIZATIONAL SCHEMES

Before you begin to collect information, you should consider the procedure's organizational scheme so that you can immediately systematize your notes and data according to the procedure's structure.

Procedures are generally organized into sections. Section titles help the user comprehend the content all the more rapidly.

Many companies do not have a standard format for their procedures, other than to write a memo on a new process or method and title it "Company Procedure." This approach is more often found in administrative areas then technical ones. One company has a handsome procedure binder with a well-designed cover. It even color-codes its procedures by type; for example, all the procedures dealing with personnel compensation are printed on green paper. Unfortunately, one turns to a procedure only to find a five- or six-page memorandum, paragraph-style, typed single-space, without a single section title or content heading to help the reader. The only recourse for the user is to skim through the numerous pages of text to determine whether he/she is using the correct procedure (because the procedure title is not as specific as it could be) or to locate the specific information he/she is seeking.

"User-friendly" is a popular term applied to computers, but it should also be applied to procedures. One way to achieve "user-friendliness" is to break down the procedure text into smaller units of information, with a system of section and subsection headings to guide the user. If these section headings can be standardized in procedures of a similar type or dealing with the same topic, all the better. The user will know what categories of information to expect and also where to locate different types of information in a procedure.

Of course, for administrative or technical procedures, the procedure's organization is largely dictated by its content. It is impossible to require the same major sections in an administrative procedure as would be needed in a maintenance procedure. As we have said, however, a company can and should standardize major sections within a procedure category, such as maintenance. When the purpose is always in Section 1, the list of tools needed is always in Section 4, and the task instructions are always in Section 6, users can more efficiently perform tasks.

2.4.1 Major Procedure Sections

Procedure sections typically found in corporate and industrial procedures are discussed below. Brevity and conciseness are goals in all procedure sections. The following discussion does not include such sections as "Discussion" or "General." This type of "catchall" section may be unsuitable because the writer may be tempted to provide lengthy background material more suited to a training manual. In the planning stage, you will determine your users' level (or levels) of training. This determination will help you provide, as briefly as possible, only enough detail to ensure that the task is performed accurately and efficiently.

Purpose (or Objective). This first section of a procedure briefly states the goal of the procedure, that is, what the procedure is intended to accomplish. It may also state why the procedure was developed, and list other, corollary purposes of the task, such as collecting data on component reliability in a procedure that deals with repairing that component.

The purpose statement should begin with the word "To." Beginning a purpose statement with "The purpose of this procedure is to" is simply redundant with the section title and is unnecessarily wordy. Here are examples of appropriate purpose statements:

Example 1

To provide guidelines to ensure the health and safety of workers exposed to hot environments.

Example 2

To establish methods for scheduling, planning, performing, and reporting internal audits.

Example 3

1.1 To provide instructions for calibrating . . .
1.2 To collect trend data on the reliability of . . .

Scope. The scope of a procedure may be approached in several ways. The scope may be considered a functional scope; that is, the scope states to which functional or personnel categories the procedure applies. The scope may also refer to systems or equipment, and would state the items of equipment the procedure covers and does not cover. Finally, the scope may summarize the activities the procedure covers. For example, the scope of a turbine operating procedure may state the modes of operation the procedure covers.

Here are some examples of scope statements:

Example 1

This procedure begins with the decision to remove obsolete materials from company stock. It covers removal from stock and disposition of the obsolete materials.

Example 2

This procedure applies to all personnel employed by Mystic Manufacturing Company.

Example 3

This procedure applies to Smith transmitter models XG1, XH1, and XI1. It does not apply to Smith transmitter models XG2 and XH2, which are covered by Procedure IE-2-065, "Smith Transmitter Calibration: XG2 and XH2."

Many organizations combine the purpose and scope sections because of the tendency toward redundancy between the two sections. For example, look again at the purpose statement example given above for the internal audit procedure. A scope statement that describes the procedure's activities would be:

> This procedure covers scheduling, planning, performing, and reporting internal audits.

You can see the redundancy between the two statements. A scope statement on the personnel responsible for internal audits, or any types of internal audits the procedure does not cover, would be more appropriate. If your procedure format includes a purpose and a scope section, the content of the scope should be specifically defined in the writing guidelines so that redundancy between the two sections is avoided.

References. A writer provides references in a procedure for different purposes:

- To maintain a record of all the source documents used in developing the procedure so that information questioned in the procedure can be verified and anyone charged with future revisions of the procedure will know the sources originally used
- To state the organization's controlling or higher level documents that require that such a procedure be in place and that it be followed (in essence, giving the procedure some "clout")

- To list other procedures or documents the user may need while performing the procedure

Your organization should determine the purpose(s) a references section should serve so that there is uniformity for the user. One method of accommodating all the above purposes is to have subsections as follows:

3.0 REFERENCES

3.1 Source Documents

The following references were used in developing this procedure:

3.2 Use References

The following references may be needed in performing this procedure:

In this format, both the sources used and the documents cited for authority are listed in Section 3.1, and the references the user may need are listed in Section 3.2.

In most organizations, a user is required to read through a procedure before starting a job or going to the work site. Thus, a user may be able to determine in advance which of the use references would be needed under the current conditions. Or, the user may need to begin performing the task before the user knows which supporting procedures are needed. The writer must determine in the planning stage whether the user has another person available to retrieve a needed procedure or whether he/she can stop the task and get it. Obviously, if the use references list is long, a user cannot be expected to carry copies of all procedures that may or may not be needed in a task.

Most plant maintenance tasks, for example, are performed by a team of at least two technicians, so one would be able to retrieve additional procedures. However, if access to the work site is poor or difficult, retrieving additional procedures may not be practical. In such a case, the writer should consider putting the needed information into the procedure rather than referencing another. A stand-alone procedure would be much easier to use in a difficult work environment. In any case, handling the need for additional procedures should be covered in training on how to use procedures.

Some organizations use the references section only for use references. The philosophy is that the user does not need to know what source documents were used to develop the procedure. To keep track of source documents used, the original writer creates a procedure history file that auditors, reviewers, or other personnel assigned to revise the procedures can review. The organization keeps these files for every procedure.

Another method of organizing references is to group them by category. This method is most often used when a great deal of source references need to be listed. For example, a power plant procedure may have the following subsections within the References section:

3.0 REFERENCES
- 3.1 Technical Specifications
- 3.2 Regulatory Documents
- 3.3 Plant Procedures
- 3.4 Plant Drawings
- 3.5 Vendor Manuals

The disadvantage of this method is that it does not tell the user which references may be needed in performing the procedure.

No matter how references are organized, the reference citation should be complete enough that any procedure user can identify and locate the document. For example, an industry code or standard should be identified not merely by number, but also by title and revision number or edition date.

Definitions. A definitions section is commonly used in administrative and higher level procedures. This section is generally not used in a technical procedure on a specific task. If the least qualified user may not understand the term, the writer defines it in the procedure text in a note. An administrative procedure may apply to all personnel in the organization, so the need for a definitions section is greater. In addition, definitions are used to convey the organization management's interpretation of a term so that all personnel understand its meaning and do not apply their own interpretation.

The terms to be defined should be listed in alphabetical order. Each term is followed by a sentence fragment defining the term. If additional explanation is required, complete sentences follow the initial definition. Here are some examples:

> Internal audit - An audit of departments under an organization's direct control that is performed by members of that organization. An internal audit may or may not be required by Quality Assurance Program requirements.
>
> Overdue finding - Any audit finding for which the required action exceeds the established due date.

Be careful to word definitions so that the procedure user can understand them. Defining a term is pointless if the definition is too complex or obscure.

Responsibilities. Like the definitions section, the responsibilities section is more commonly found in administrative procedures. This section should identify the particular personnel (by functional title) charged with implementing the procedural requirements.

A technical procedure does not normally need a responsibilities section because the responsibilities, if not implicit, can be delineated in the action steps. For example, a maintenance procedure is written for a maintenance technician (or team of technicians). It is implicit that this technician is responsible for performing the procedure correctly. Moreover, anytime an additional personnel category is needed, it is stated in other procedure sections, such as "Prerequisites," (obtain Maintenance Supervisor's approval before starting work) or the action steps themselves (notify Chemistry Department to take a water sample).

A responsibilities section is needed in an administrative or higher level document that involves several personnel groups or departments to accomplish the procedure's purpose. For example, a procedure controlling heavy loads handling and lifting may list the following responsibilities:

> The Plant Manager ensures the implementation of the Heavy Loads Handling Program.
>
> The Engineering Supervisor provides direction and guidance in developing procedures and design changes concerning heavy loads handling.
>
> The Maintenance Supervisor ensures that all repairs, inspections, tests, and servicing of lifting equipment are accomplished.

The key to a succinct, concise responsibilities section is level of detail. Remember, the instructions themselves will delineate the specific tasks along with who is to perform them. A responsibilities section should not go into great detail because it will merely result in repeating the instructions. Use the responsibilities section for a more global statement of the personnel involved and their function with regard to this procedure.

Another point concerning succinct wording in this section. You will recall that we recommend beginning a purpose statement with "To" to avoid redundant wording. Similarly, avoid wording such as the following in the responsibilities section:

Too Wordy:

4.0 RESPONSIBILITIES

4.1 The Plant Manager is responsible for ensuring the implementation of . . .

OR

4.1 It is the responsibility of the Plant Manager to ensure the implementation of . . .

Instead, use the following wording to avoid redundancy with the section title:

Concise:

The Plant Manager ensures . . .

OR

The Plant Manager shall ensure . . .

System Description. A technical procedure on operation, maintenance, or testing of equipment or a system may contain this section. A system description should be a brief discussion of one or two paragraphs that gives the user an overview of the system on which he/she will be working. This section may also discuss how work on this system affects other systems. The procedure writer must guard against developing a lengthy discussion here. Procedure users tell us that the brevity of the discussion directly correlates with the time or inclination they have to read the section.

Prerequisites. This section identifies actions or procedures that must be completed before procedure use. It should also identify, where applicable, plant conditions that must exist before procedure use. This section implies that the user must verify all prerequisites are met before he/she begins the procedure. Some organizations require a signoff to ensure all prerequisites are verified. Typical prerequisites include:

- Completion of documents, tasks, or other procedures
- Requirements for work approvals
- Requirements for work orders or permits
- Initial conditions to be established, such as system isolation
- Availability or operability of needed equipment
- Special communications requirements

The prerequisites section should not be used for any safety-related requirements. The precautions section, discussed below, covers safety issues.

A procedure covering several different tasks may have different prerequisites that come into play as the user begins each task.

Prerequisites that only apply to certain procedure sections may be handled two ways:

- The prerequisites for a given section are presented in that section, either as the first heading of the section, or as the first action steps.
- All prerequisites are listed in the prerequisites section in the front of the procedure, but the section to which a prerequisite applies is specifically identified.

Of the two methods above, the first is preferable because the information is physically located where the user will need it. The more prerequisites listed in the front of the procedure, the greater the chance that the user will not remember them when he/she reaches the section to which they apply. In addition, if a signoff is required for a section-specific prerequisite, the user will avoid a backward reference if the prerequisites are located at the beginning of the appropriate section.

Here are some examples of typical prerequisites that are phrased as user instructions:

> Obtain Maintenance Order for insulation removal and installation.
>
> Verify the air heaters are in service.

The following prerequisites are phrased as accomplished facts or conditions. User verification is implicit.

> Forced draft fan room is clear of debris.
>
> Procedure Temporary Change Notice has been issued and approved by Department Supervisor.

The following are examples of presenting prerequisites within the procedure instructional section:

4. Turning Gear Operation

   4.1 Prerequisites

      4.1.1 Oil flow to the generator seals has been established.

4.1.2 Turbine Lube Oil System is operating in accordance with SOP 2200/06, "Turbine Lube Oil System Operation."

Section 4.1 completed by ______ Date ______

4.2 Placing the Unit on Gear

4.2.1 Start the Turning Gear Oil Pump . . .

Signoffs for prerequisites are positioned in one of three places:

- Immediately after each prerequisite (used where each prerequisite is extremely critical)
- At the end of the prerequisites section (one signoff indicating that all have been performed or verified)
- On a data sheet

Precautions. Statements given in this section alert the user to important measures that should be used to protect personnel from injury and equipment from damage. Precautions also alert the user to conditions or actions that might cause plant downtime, abnormal situations, or emergencies.

Precautions are limited to cautionary statements that are global in nature; that is, they apply to the procedure as a whole or they must be known before the procedure is begun. Cautionary statements applicable to specific steps or sections of a procedure should be located just before the applicable step or section. As mentioned above for prerequisites, the more precautions given in the front of the procedure, the greater the chance that one or more of them will not be remembered. Therefore, if any statement is not global in application, it should be located in the instructional section where it applies.

Precautions in industrial and power plant procedures include:

- Requirements for handling hazardous material
- Requirements such as special clothing for dealing with hazardous environments such as high temperatures, high pressures, high voltages, and toxic or flammable gases
- Precautions concerning procedure actions that may affect plant safety or availability

Here are examples of precautions from technical procedures:

> *DO NOT* repack valves while they are under pressure without the approval of a Group Supervisor.
>
> When working in radiologically controlled areas, treat all fluids and materials as contaminated unless certified radiologically clean by Radiation Control.
>
> Use caution when working around energized components.

Materials Needed. This section is used in any procedure requiring specific materials, tools, or equipment. The section may be named appropriately for the type of procedure. Examples are:

- Materials Needed
- Special Tools
- Special Equipment
- Repair Parts

Some plants have separate sections for tools and for repair parts, for example. Normally, a section on special tools would list only those not found in a technician's standard tool kit.

Personnel Requirements. This section is used to specify the number and functional title of personnel needed to perform the task. This section is most appropriate for certain technical procedures, such as those dealing with repair, maintenance, or testing.

Procedure. This section presents the action step instructions to perform the task. The structure of this section is determined in planning, and is reflected in the expanded outline. The procedure section follows the structure of that outline. This section may also be called "Instructions."

Restoration. This section is used in technical procedures, particularly maintenance. Typically, a piece of equipment must be removed from service to be tested or worked on. The restoration section gives instructions for returning the equipment to service. Sometimes restoration instructions are not given a separate section, but are the last subsection of the "Procedure" section.

Acceptance Criteria. A technical procedure on testing or maintenance will need to have acceptance criteria that tell the technician whether the results of the test or the maintenance activity are acceptable. Acceptance criteria may be presented in a separate section, particularly if there is one final overall result to be achieved. Sometimes, this section is placed before the "Procedure" section. However, a task may have many acceptance criteria as the user works through it. In this case, these criteria are presented within the procedure steps or on a data sheet or both.

Attachments. This section lists the material attached to the procedure by attachment number and title. Attachments to procedures are sometimes called enclosures, or more specifically categorized by type—figures, tables, checklists, data sheets, and appendixes.

This procedure section is not needed if the procedure has a "List of Effective Pages" or a table of contents. The procedure user needs to be able to check whether the procedure contains all the attachments it should, so one of these three methods is needed.

2.4.2 Typical Sections Used in Procedures

The many possible procedure sections described above are not appropriate for all procedures. The following examples show the sections used in various procedure types:

- Administrative Procedure
  - 1.0 Purpose
  - 2.0 Scope
  - 3.0 Definitions
  - 4.0 References
  - 5.0 Responsibilities
  - 6.0 Instructions

7.0 Records
8.0 Attachments

- Mechanical Maintenance Procedure
  1.0 Purpose
  2.0 References
  3.0 Personnel Requirements
  4.0 Precautions
  5.0 Prerequisites
  6.0 Special Tools
  7.0 Procedure
  8.0 Acceptance Requirements
  9.0 Restoration
  10.0 Attachments
- System Operating Procedure
  1.0 Purpose
  2.0 References
  3.0 System Description
  4.0 Precautions
  5.0 System Startup
    5.1 Prerequisites
    5.2 Instructions
  6.0 Normal Operation
    6.1 Prerequisites
    6.2 Instructions
  7.0 System Shutdown
    7.1 Prerequisites
    7.2 Instructions
  8.0 Attachments

2.5 A SYSTEM FOR NOTE TAKING AND ORGANIZING THE COLLECTED INFORMATION

As described in the next section, a writer will collect and analyze a great deal of information during the planning stage. While analyzing this information the writer must make many critical decisions that will affect the usefulness of the procedure. The writer must decide which information to use, which to discard, and which bits of information from different sources are related. This research process often requires the writer to develop a comprehensive set of notes that then must be analyzed again before beginning to write the procedure.

The trick to becoming an efficient procedure writer is to begin to think of the final product as soon as possible in the writing process. This emphasis on developing the final product begins with establishing a system for organizing notes during the research phase. Thus, the writer has a set of notes organized in the same sequence as the final procedure. This process saves the writer the additional step of having to organize a large volume of notes at the end of the research phase.

The system described below allows the writer to organize the information analyzed as it relates to the organization of the final procedure. Think of a procedure as having three parts: front matter, instructions, and back matter.

The front matter of a procedure contains all the sections of the procedure that precede the instructions, such as Purpose, Responsibilities, Precautions, and Special Tools. The instructions are the detailed tasks, steps, and substeps a user needs to perform to accomplish the procedure's purpose. The back matter follows the instructions and usually contains figures, forms, data sheets, and the like.

The procedure writer collects and analyzes information from several sources. The information may belong in the front matter, instructions, or back matter. Without having a system to organize the notes, you will have to review the notes again when developing the first draft of the procedure.

Before starting your research, set up a filing system to match the final format of the procedure. The complexity of the procedure will determine the completeness of the filing system. Some writers begin with a separate sheet of paper for each major section of the procedure. The section sheets are then organized in a file folder for each of the three major units, for example, front matter. Others begin with a separate file folder for each procedure section.

As you research and analyze the information and decide the appropriate location for the information you are going to use, immediately place this information on the appropriate sheet of paper or in the appropriate file folder. Continue this process throughout the research phase. Your goal is to have an organized database of information at the end of the research phase. This organized database will expedite the drafting of the procedure.

Approaching the writing task with a clear picture of the final product helps reduce the time needed to draft the procedure. Consider how much time the writer would save by using the organized note-taking and filing system in the following example.

Example

A writer must analyze a vendor's manual to develop a new procedure for removing and restoring a piece of equipment from service. The writer would glean information from the manual and organize it as follows:

- The title of the manual and associated information would be added to Section 2.0, References.
- The writer would use the information in the manual to develop the removal and restoration subsections of Section 6.0, Instructions. By developing the two subsections concurrently, the writer avoids the problem of developing inconsistent steps for the two subsections.
- From another document the writer knows that when equipment is removed or restored to service, an independent verification is required. Thus, for Section 8.0, Attachments, the writer jots a note to include a signoff for the two subsections on a data sheet.
- The writer also determines that an illustration is needed for both the removal and restoration of the equipment, so he/she makes a rough sketch and then meets with graphic support personnel to arrange for the illustration to be completed by the time the draft is developed. The

writer then places a copy of the rough sketch in the Section 8.0 file.

If this process is followed throughout the procedure research phase, the writer will have assembled all the procedure content in the appropriate sequence.

2.6 COLLECTING INFORMATION

The writer collects information in two broad categories: technical (or content) information and user information. Both types of information are needed because a procedure must be both technically accurate and written and formatted so that the user can comprehend and perform the procedure. A technically accurate procedure that cannot be understood by the user is an ineffective procedure. On the other hand, a well written, user-friendly procedure with technical errors in it can cause serious consequences in the environment in which it is performed.

As you collect information, you should be developing the following written products:

- A revised purpose statement and title, if necessary
- A topic outline of major tasks involved in the procedure
- Notes on procedure content, which should then be filed in the appropriate folder.

These products will be used later in the planning stage to develop the final planning product.

2.6.1 Technical Information

Writing a new procedure or a revision requires collecting a great deal of information. You are responsible for collecting the most accurate, up-to-date source material. You must gather the latest revisions of all the technical information you collect to ensure that accurate information is put into your procedure. Moreover, you should keep an up-to-date list of the sources you use because these will need to be included in the references section of the procedure or in a procedure history file.

The technical information to be collected depends on the subject of the procedure. Any of the following types of information may be appropriate:

- For administrative procedures:
  - Corporate policies
  - Related or similar procedures
  - Related correspondence and memoranda
  - Instructional and user's manuals (for example, those dealing with the corporate computer system)
  - Related forms
  - Regulatory documents
  - Related training materials
  - Documentation on previous procedure changes (if you are revising an existing procedure)
- For technical procedures:
  - Engineering drawings and sketches
  - Vendor operating and maintenance manuals for equipment
  - System descriptions
  - Technical Specifications
  - Spare parts lists
  - Similar or related procedures
  - Related correspondence (internal or from manufacturers)
  - Training department materials, such as lesson plans, student guides, and examinations on the operation of equipment
  - Documentation on previous procedure changes (if you are revising an existing procedure)

In addition to collecting documentation, you may find it helpful to interview an experienced person to identify potential problem areas with the task or the equipment.

You need to consider the following factors while collecting technical information:

Tasks Required. Your first step in developing the topic outline we mentioned above is to identify the major tasks needed to accomplish the procedure's purpose. Identify and make note of these tasks as you perform your research. Once you identify them, arrange them in a tentative sequence. (You will analyze task sequence in further detail later in planning.) As you continue further in the planning stage, you will identify steps and substeps to support these tasks.

The major tasks identified should name an activity the user must perform, for example, disassembly of the system component. Another factor, task characteristics, must also be considered, as described immediately below.

Task Characteristics. As you review your source documents, make note of any critical characteristics of the tasks in your topic outline. Such characteristics include:

- Frequency of the task (Is it required to be performed at certain intervals?)
- Cautionary information that the user needs, or anything related to safety
- Requirements for special materials, forms, tools, and the like
- Inspection and testing points and requirements
- Acceptance criteria for a testing task
- Training considerations (Is a certain level of personnel required to perform this task?)
- Major decision points
- Prerequisites and preparations that must be done before the task

Task characteristics such as those listed above should be kept in mind as you collect and analyze technical information.

2.6.2 User Information

As we said earlier, a technically accurate procedure is ineffective if it cannot be performed by the user. One way to help ensure that the procedure can be performed by the intended user(s) is to gather as much information about that user as we can.

Two types of user information you should collect are readability factors and task-related factors. Readability factors are further divided into the user, the document, and the environment, and task-related factors include the task frequency, complexity, criticality, and time limit (if any).

Readability Factors. The term readability has often been used as a measure of the ease or difficulty of reading of a particular document. Selections that are difficult to read are considered to have a high readability level; those that are easy to read have a low readability level. The basic premise for this concept relates to the fact that people will comprehend more if a document has a low readability level.

Contrary to the preachings of some reading experts, there is no readability formula that will tell a writer the vocabulary level and sentence length that will be needed to guarantee that all users of a procedure will be able to comprehend. Readability is a dynamic concept consisting of the interaction among the reader (user), the document or medium being read, and the environment in which the reading and comprehension are taking place.

- **The User**. Variables related to the user are:

  Purpose and Motivation. A user will put forth the intellectual energy required to comprehend a procedure when the user has a clear purpose for reading the procedure and the motivation to perform the task. If a user does not perceive a task to be useful, he/she may not perform the task well. However, when the user understands the purpose and the results or importance of the task, he/she is more likely to put more effort into comprehending and performing the procedure correctly.

- **Training and Experience**. Each user has a unique level of training and experience. You should determine the skills and knowledge taught in training so that you know the level of the least qualified person who will perform the task. You may also want to consult with the personnel or human resources department to determine the number of years of experience your users have. Again, it is the user with the fewest years of experience to whom you should write, not to an average experience level.

  The effect of practice should also be considered. Do not assume that because a skill has been learned in training it will stay with the person year in, year out. A skill must be reinforced by periodic correct practice or it will deteriorate. This fact affects routine and nonroutine tasks. A routine task may be performed incorrectly because the user tends to rely more on memory than on the written procedure. For a non-routine task that is performed infrequently, the user will probably be more careful to follow the written procedure.

- **Knowledge of Content**. A procedure is more readable if the user understands the technical information presented. For example, an engineer will have less difficulty understanding a procedure on design control than the engineering department clerk. However, if both must use the procedure, it must be written so that both can understand the content.

• **The Document**. Variables related to the document are:

  - **Procedure Format**. A user expects to find a procedure developed in a specific format. For example, the "Purpose" section might always be the first section. In addition to expecting the procedure sections to be in the same sequence, the user also expects the type of information contained in each section to be appropriate for that particular section.

When a user comes across a different format or does not find the expected information in a section, the probability of a communication or comprehension error increases. The procedure writer must ensure that the standard format for the particular type of procedure being written is followed, and—just as important—ensure that the information contained in the section is appropriate.

The user of a procedure has every right to expect that when a section title states "Responsibilities," only responsibilities will be discussed, not information that belongs in another section of the procedure. Performance errors caused by the writer not following the dictates of the content requirements of a section can have serious and costly consequences.

For example, a company's policy was that all cautionary information applicable to the entire procedure should appear in a section titled "Precautions" and that cautionary information applicable to a specific step or series of steps should be placed immediately before the applicable step(s). In one procedure the writer included information that was step specific in the "Precautions" section. The user read the information and proceeded to perform the procedure. Six hours into the task, the step to which the cautionary information applied was performed, but the user did not remember this information from the "Precautions" section. As a result, critical equipment was damaged, and personnel faced the potential for serious injury. The damage cost the company more than $24 million in downtime before the equipment was repaired. This problem may have been avoided had the writer followed the company policy of inserting step-specific cautionary information at the appropriate step instead of expecting the reader to retain such information throughout the procedure.

- **Procedure Organization**. The format considerations discussed above in a sense are related to organization, but organization within the instructional sections of the procedure where tasks and steps must be presented in a logical order is most critical. When a user discovers the steps are not in the logical order in which the task should be accomplished, he/she begins to question the validity of the procedure itself and then must interpret how the procedure should be performed.
- **Level of Detail**. You must constantly decide on the level of detail needed. These decisions are made on the global level (what tasks should be included) and the specific level (how much detail should be included at each step). If a user has to interpret the information by asking, for example, a "How?" question, then enough detail has not been presented. However, providing a "cookbook" or too much detail can adversely affect readability. A user will skip over items that are too detailed and may miss critical information.
- **Document Design Features**. You may not realize that document design features such as the spacing between lines and the indentation of subsections are not merely for "looks," but have definite human factors based reasons for their inclusion in a procedure. For example, a user has difficulty finding the beginnings and ends of sections or steps when a procedure is double spaced throughout. Different spacing within steps and between steps makes the procedure much easier to read. Similarly, indentation of sublevels tells the user what kind of step he/she will be reading, a higher level one or a detailed substep.
- **Concept Load and Concept Density**. Concept load refers to the number of ideas presented in a unit, such as a sentence or paragraph. In procedures, the unit

is a step. A high concept load, that is, numerous ideas or actions in one step, puts heavy demands on the reader/user and risks performance errors. Concept density refers to the number of times these high-concept-load steps appear in a procedure. Obviously, a high concept load coupled with a high concept density is to be avoided in procedure writing. The ideal concept load is one action per step, and in a 56-step procedure, the ideal concept density would be 56. Criteria for the number of action verbs per step are discussed in detail in Chapter 3.

- **Writing Style**. For the fewest performance errors related to procedures, your writing style should place minimal demands on the reader. For the user to understand and perform the procedure, the writing style should match his/her language ability. A clear writing style with short sentences and commonly used vocabulary will help ensure that your procedure is performed without error. Writing style and vocabulary are discussed in detail in Chapter 3.

- **The Environment of Use**. Environment plays an important part in the successful performance of a procedure. You should know the conditions under which the procedure will be performed. In the review stage, you will walk through a procedure to determine its compatibility with the user and the worksite. Now, you can walk through the procedure or talk with users to determine environmental considerations such as the following:
  - Is the site accessible?
  - Are hazards present? If so, do they require precautions or should the procedure tasks be changed? Consider such hazards as heights, noise, obstacles, heat, high humidity, toxic gases, and high voltages.
  - Does the procedure require that awkward body positions be held for a long time?

- Are there any potential problems with visual considerations, such as glare or poor lighting?
- Are protective devices or clothing needed and do they hinder performance?
- Does protective clothing interfere with communication between users?
- Does the procedure require travel between different buildings? If so, does the user have access to transportation?
- Does the user have access to equipment needed to perform the procedure (for example, is special clearance needed to use a computer)?

The environmental considerations listed above can place stress upon the user. There are two kinds of stressors, physiological and psychological. Physiological stressors include:

- Duration of stress
- Fatigue
- Pain or discomfort
- Temperature extremes
- Oxygen insufficiency
- Vibration
- Loud noises

Psychological stressors include:

- Task speed
- High risk
- Monotonous work
- Sensory deprivation
- Distractions (noise, glare, movement, conversation)

You should determine what environmental considerations and the resultant stress placed on the user apply to your procedure. Addressing these considerations now, in planning, will result in a smoother, briefer review stage.

Task-Related Factors. In addition to the readability factors discussed above, the following factors related to the task have an effect on the level of detail you need to provide and on the user's ability to perform the procedure correctly.

- **Task Frequency**. The frequency of a task has implications for the level of detail that should be provided, but not in the manner you might suppose. A task performed yearly should have a high level of detail; however, a task performed weekly should not necessarily have only a low level of detail. The key is who is to perform the procedure. A weekly procedure may not be performed by the same person every week, and therefore may need more details. You should analyze the users involved in the task to determine the appropriate level of detail for a task that is performed frequently.
- **Task Complexity**. Complex tasks are more likely to be performed inaccurately or incompletely than simple, short tasks. If you are highly experienced in a complex task, you should guard against omitting steps in the process that may be second nature to you. They may not be second nature to the user. Interviewing users, both experienced and inexperienced, will give you an idea of what level of detail is needed. Where large numbers of actions are involved, a system of checkoffs may be needed to help the user keep his/her place in the sequence.
- **Task Criticality**. If incorrect performance could cause a serious consequence such as personnel injury, equipment damage, or plant downtime, provide a high level of detail to ensure that the task is performed correctly. Your most important consideration in determining level of detail is whether errors of omission (skipping a step) or commission (performing a step incorrectly or out of sequence) will result in serious consequences.

- **Time Limit**. If a task must be completed within a certain time limit, level of detail is important. If the procedure has too few details, the time the user spends searching for needed information may threaten his/her ability to perform the procedure within the time limit. However, if the procedure has too many details, the increased time needed to simply read the procedure may make it impossible to perform the procedure within the specified time.

At this point, you should have collected many types of technical information, considered readability and task-related factors that affect the user, and loosely organized this information into a system of file folders that correspond to the major sections of the procedure. You should also have a purpose statement, title (both revised if necessary), and a topic outline of the major tasks in the procedure. Now you are ready to analyze and organize the information you have collected.

2.7 ANALYZING AND ORGANIZING INFORMATION

This step essentially consists of two tasks:

- Reviewing your system of file folders to analyze and organize your notes, deleting and expanding as necessary
- Revising and expanding your topic outline to a much more detailed level, the expanded outline

The approaches and techniques discussed below should help you accomplish these tasks. The written products you develop in this step are a series of more and more detailed planning products until you have the final planning product, the expanded outline. We will discuss exactly what is an expanded outline later in this chapter. First, let's consider two initial approaches to analyzing and organizing your collected information.

2.7.1 Inputs, Methods, and Results: A Framework for Analyzing Information

You will recall that earlier in this chapter we discussed two ways of organizing file folders for your notes—by individual procedure section or by front matter, instructions, and back matter. The three components of the latter method can be viewed as follows:

- Front matter includes the **inputs** to the task or process described in the procedure.
- The instructions are the **method** for accomplishing the task.
- Back matter usually deals with the **results** (or outputs) of the task. The exception is the supplemental material you wish to include as an attachment. It does not strictly have to do with the results of the task.

Inputs. Inputs are those actions or conditions that would initiate the procedure's use or that should be done before beginning the procedural task, such as:

- What will originate the need for the task?
- How will the need for the task be known and recognized?
- What must have occurred before performing the task? Consider materials, equipment, documents, activities, and plant conditions.
- What must the user assemble to perform the task? Consider tools, equipment, and materials; documentation such as forms; other procedures; and verification of plant conditions or equipment status.

Method. The method is essentially "how" the task is to be accomplished, but includes more than just the instructions. Method includes:

- Instructions on how to do the task
- Safety or cautionary information the user needs while performing the task
- Supplemental or explanatory information that would help the user perform the task
- Inspections, verifications, and approvals needed while the task is ongoing

Results. The results include the information and documentation the user will need to determine whether the task was performed correctly or to document the task results. Results include:

- Acceptance criteria
- Data sheets to record the results of the task
- Forms that must be completed by the user and approved by another person to document the task was accomplished
- Illustrations, graphs, and tables the user may need to determine whether the appropriate results have been achieved. As you analyze and organize your information, keep in mind this framework of inputs, method, and results.

2.7.2 A Technique for Revising and Expanding the Topic Outline

You already have a broad topic outline, which was your first cut at the scope and sequence of the procedure. You probably wrote this outline on a single sheet of paper. Using the technique described below, you will create an outline that is a lot easier to work with than that single sheet of paper.

This technique uses strips of paper, index cards, or glue-backed squares of paper. Write each item in your topic outline on a strip of paper and arrange the strips in the logical sequence for performance of the procedure. You may want to look at several options as to how the tasks should be sequenced, so you can rearrange the strips at will. Next, for each task, decide on steps and substeps needed and jot them on additional strips of paper. Now arrange all the strips in the appropriate sequence. You should indent the step and substep strips so that the structure is visually clear. At this point, if you have determined any cautionary or explanatory information, you can insert it in the sequence also.

This technique has two advantages:

- It forces you to focus on the task/step/substep hierarchy needed
- Because the strips are movable, you have the opportunity to try out different organizational schemes without investing a great deal of time in rewriting outlines. Once a writer commits a sequence to a format such as an outline or flowchart structure, the writer will be less likely to make critical structural changes because of the need to rewrite.

This technique is well suited to creating a flowchart of the procedure, whether the final product will be a flowchart or whether you prefer a flowchart to an outline to organize the ideas and sequence. Each strip of paper corresponds to a symbol on the flowchart.

2.7.3 Developing the Expanded Outline

The expanded outline will be the final product of the planning stage. However, you must develop it continuously as you analyze and organize information. If you use the technique described in Section 2.7.2, you will have an outline or flowchart of the correct step sequence. As you review the information you have collected and added to your file folders, you will add this information to the outline/flowchart. In addition, you should begin to draft the noninstructional sections. Finally, you will be identifying the need for graphics, such as illustrations or data sheets.

The expanded outline is the final product resulting from performing the above. In short, as you analyze and organize information, you should be building an expanded outline that consists of:

- Noninstructional sections in draft form
- An outline or flowchart of instructional section(s)
- Preliminary graphics

This outline, as you can see, is very close to a complete procedure draft. If at the end of your planning stage you have an expanded outline as described above, then the drafting stage consists mainly of formatting, drafting your outline/flowchart of steps, and refining the graphics.

The sections below discuss aspects of procedure planning that you need to consider as you develop the topic outline into an expanded outline.

2.7.4 Task Structuring: Subordination and Coordination

We discussed above creating an outline or flowchart using movable strips of paper. That is the method; now to what ideas do we apply the method? Your procedure may contain one or more tasks, each of which requires several steps and substeps, and perhaps even more detailed sub-substeps. You must decide which tasks, steps, and substeps are coordinated with each other and which are subordinate to others.

Coordination simply means that ideas, or in this case tasks or steps, are of equal weight or importance. Coordinate ideas are for example, Steps 1 and 2 of a process. Subordination means that one idea is of lesser weight or importance, or it supports another idea. Step 2.1 of a procedure is subordinate to Step 2. These concepts may seem obvious, but we have seen task structures where steps and substeps of unequal weight are not structured properly.

You already have the main ideas or topics in your topic outline. If you have covered your procedure's scope completely, then you will now be assigning subordinate ideas or steps to these main ideas. Then, you may need to go one or two levels further to describe substeps and sub-substeps. If you do not have a complete topic outline, then you may still need to add more coordinate ideas to the outline. In either case, one of the reasons for the movable strips of paper is so that you are not locked into one technical sequence of topics. At any point you may add, delete, or change the order of topics as needed.

As you are using our suggested technique to more fully develop your topic outline, be very conscious of the concepts of coordination and subordination and be sure that substeps are truly substeps and not independent steps of equal weight. Look at the following example where the writer did not structure coordinate and subordinate ideas properly:

Example of Incorrect Task Structuring

6.0 PROCEDURE

6.1 Notify Shift Supervisor before beginning test.

6.1.1 Test Set-up

6.1.1.1 Substep

6.1.1.2 Substep

6.1.1.3 Substep

6.1.2 Loop Test

6.1.2.1 Apply the following inputs with the simulators. Record obtained values on Data Sheet 1.

6.1.2.2 Vary each input separately as for input 1 in the table above while holding the other three inputs at 0.5 VDC. Record obtained values on Data Sheet 1.

6.1.3 If all values are within tolerance, return loop to service as follows:

(Substep)

6.1.4 If all values are *NOT* within tolerance, calibrate per Procedure IC.2.1.

This writer gets into trouble with the second step. The "Test Set-up" task is not subordinate to notifying the supervisor. Rather, it is a second step, and should be numbered 6.2. As a result, all the remaining steps are subordinated and numbered incorrectly. An additional problem occurs at Step 6.1.3. Returning the loop to service is not part of the test. It is a separate task.

Below is the same procedure segment restructured:

Example of Correct Task Structuring

6.0 PROCEDURE

6.1 Notify Shift Supervisor before beginning test.

6.2 Set up test as follows:
 6.2.1 Substep
 6.2.2 Substep
 6.2.3 Substep

6.3 Conduct loop test as follows:
 6.3.1 Apply the following inputs with the simulators. Record obtained values on Data Sheet 1.
 6.3.2 Vary each input separately as for input 1 in the table above while holding the other three inputs at 0.5 VDC. Record obtained values on Data Sheet 1.
 6.3.3 If all values are within tolerance, go to Step 6.4.
 6.3.4 If all values are *NOT* within tolerance, calibrate per Procedure IC.2.1.

6.4 Return loop to service as follows:
 (substeps)

You can see that this restructuring has the added benefit of eliminating the need to place substeps at the four-digit (6.1.1.1) level.

Thus, proper task structuring is important because it helps the user see the logic of the instructions and how they are related to each other.

2.7.5 Deductive Structure

Related to the concepts of coordination and subordination is deductive structure. A deductive structure is one in which the main ideas are presented first, and then are supported by details. Applying this concept to your planning product, the outline or flowchart, helps you structure tasks correctly. A properly constructed planning product is an example of good deductive structure, because each major section contains supporting details. The procedure section may contain several levels of details, arranged deductively.

Deductive structure will be discussed further as it applies to paragraphing in Chapter 3.

2.7.6 Level of Detail and Message Elements

As stated previously, a major decision a procedure writer must make is deciding on the appropriate level of detail for the intended users of the procedure. This decision affects the entire content. The decision will affect the number of tasks developed in the instructions section of the procedure, the number of steps and substeps needed to be developed for each task, and the quantity and type of graphics needed to help the intended user accomplish the tasks.

A useful way to decide on the level of detail is to consider the message elements that need to be included. The major message elements to consider are **what, how, when, where, who, and why.**

- The **what** elements are the tasks to be performed.
- The **how** elements detail the actions to achieve the tasks.
- **When** elements are considered in two phases. First, the stated sequence of the tasks and steps tells the user the appropriate sequence of performance. In addition, there will be steps that must be completed at a specific time or when a specific condition is met, such as, "When the tank level reaches 14 feet, close valve."
- The **who** element is used when the main procedure user is not the person intended to perform the task. For example, a procedure would not have an appropriate level of detail if it directed a user to perform an action that the user is not responsible for performing or is not allowed to perform. For example, a step that stated "Enter values on computer Y" was written in a procedure. As stated, the main user would have to enter the values into the computer. In actual practice, however, the user was not allowed to enter any data into the computer. Thus, to be correct, the step should have stated "Contact data processing to enter values on computer Y."

- **Where** elements are used when the writer decides the user needs specific location information. For example, the **where** element is needed in a procedure that requires the user to complete a form. Additional guidance on location information is in Chapter 3.
- **Why** elements explain the reasons a particular task or step is being performed. A word of caution about **why** elements: A procedure writer must resist the temptation of explaining all the possible **why** elements that could be included in a procedure. As a general rule, detailed **why** elements should be reserved for training manuals.

The decision as to a procedure's level of detail begins at the task level. The procedure must contain the appropriate number of tasks to ensure that the intended users are able to accomplish the procedure's purpose. For example, a procedure that contains a task to remove a component from service but is missing a task to return it to service does not have the appropriate detail at the task level.

After deciding on the appropriate detail at the task level, the writer moves to the step and substep levels (if any) for each task. The writer must ensure that each task contains the appropriate steps and substeps to perform the task as intended. Then, the appropriate level of detail must be considered for each step and substep developed.

Consider the following decision-making process that could be used for the example given. For the purpose of this discussion, the levels of detail are defined as a range from gross (the least amount of detail) to fine (the most amount of detail).

Level of Detail	Step
GROSS	Isolate letdown line.

The writer decided that the least experienced, qualified user has the knowledge and skills to isolate the letdown line. Notice that the verb "isolate" is a function verb; that is, a number of actions must be performed to achieve isolation of the letdown line.

Level of Detail	Step
LOW	Isolate letdown line by closing valves C-14 and C-16.

Here the writer decided that the user needed an additional level of detail to isolate the letdown line. The writer added a **how** element of information. Notice that the action verb "close" is now "by closing" in the middle of the sentence. This type of step could also be written as "Close valves C-14 and C-16 to isolate letdown line." In this case, the message elements change by their placement in the sentence. As shown below, in the first example, the function verb "isolate" serves as a **what** element; in the second example, the phrase "to isolate" serves as a **why** element.

WHAT / HOW

Isolate letdown line by closing valves C-14 and C-16.

HOW / WHY

Close valves V-14 and V-16 to isolate letdown line.

As a rule of thumb, it is preferable to begin the step statement with the verb that most directly describes the physical or mental action, followed by the function (why or what).

The writer could then ask, "Does the user know where the valves are located?" If location information is needed, the step would be written as:

Level of Detail	Step
MEDIUM	Close valves C-14 and C-16 on Panel 18 to isolate letdown line.

The writer would then decide whether the message element **when** is needed for the user. If **when** information is related to a condition, such as a specific pressure, the step would be written as:

Level of Detail	Step
HIGH	When the pressure increases to 150 psig, close valves C-14 and C-16 on Panel 18 to isolate letdown line.

When information is also added to a step when time is a factor, such as:

> "After the unit has been operating 30 minutes, close valves . . ."

The writer may then ask the question, "Does the user know how to close the valves?" If the writer decides that the user needs additional information, another level of **how** information would be added:

Level of Detail	Step
FINE	When pressure increases to 150 psig, close valves C-14 and C-16 on Panel 18 by turning the handwheel counterclockwise to isolate letdown line.

This decision-making process continues for each step in the procedure until the writer decides that the appropriate level of detail is achieved for the intended user(s).

2.7.7 Considering Decision Points

As you outline or chart the procedure steps, you may come across decision points for the user. At these points, the decision made determines the direction the user will take in the following steps. For example, if one of two identical pieces of equipment is not operating, the user's decision may be simple, to use the other piece of equipment. However, if an instrument cannot be calibrated to within a certain tolerance range, the user must decide whether to continue attempting to calibrate or to stop and notify a supervisor. Another example of a decision point would be the many responses that must be made to changing conditions during a plant emergency. An emergency procedure may contain several divergent paths that are followed depending on conditions. The decision load is understandably heavy in such procedures, and for that reason, many nuclear power plants are turning to flowcharts rather than prose for emergency procedures, because the decisions and the subsequent paths to follow are graphically and clearly presented by symbols, flow paths, and arrowheads.

For each decision point in your procedure, consider the following elements:

Who. You should consider whether the user or other personnel, such as a supervisor or a technical support person, should make the decision. If a certain level of qualified personnel is required to make the decision, you should specify it in the procedure.

Documentation. Consider whether the decision made needs to be documented. Generally, decisions users make in the course of performing a task do not need special documentation. It is the nonroutine decision that should generally be documented. In addition, decisions made by other personnel are generally supported by a signoff in the procedure because they usually concern approval of an action or result of a task.

2.7.8 Verifications and Approvals

Certain procedure steps may need to be verified as done correctly. A verification can be performed by the user (self-verification) or by an independent verifier (an inspector or supervisor, for example). Approvals are needed for managerial controls and to allow further action to be taken.

For those tasks or steps requiring verification or approval, determine the following:

- The purpose to be achieved
- Who should verify or approve
- The method that should be used to document the verification or approval

Depending on the purpose of the verification or approval, you can use one of several methods to document it:

Checkoffs. Checkoffs are used to help the user monitor work progress or keep his/her place in a series of actions. A small blank line is placed at the end of each step for the user to place a check mark. This technique is especially helpful for long lists of actions or objects of actions such as a list of valves that must be lined up.

It is preferable to place the checkoff blank as shown in Example 1 below rather than as shown in Example 2.

Example 1: Preferred Placement of Checkoff

Turn on the synchroscope for the reserve feed breaker to Bus 45. Verify the synchroscope locks in the in-phase position.

____

Example 2: Less Effective Placement of Checkoff

________ Turn on the synchroscope for the reserve feed breaker to Bus 45. Verify the synchroscope locks in the in-phase position.

In Example 1, the checkoff placement on the right follows our reading pattern, from left to right and down the page. In Example 2, the user must read the step and then return to the beginning of the step to check it off. This placement requires the user to move slightly backward in the procedure. Another problem with this placement of the checkoff is that the user tends to read the first action in the step, check it off, and move on, while the step has a second action, "Verify," in the second sentence.

Your organization may require that all checkoff blanks be checked off, or it may take the position that they are there in case the user needs them as a self-verification or a placekeeping aid. Checkoffs are the lowest level of verification method.

Signoffs. A signoff is used to document a higher level of verification, either self or independent. A signoff is also used to document approval. The user, or another person who is verifying or approving, initials the space provided to indicate the step has been performed correctly. A signoff may require a signature instead of initials; it may also require a date. Usually, the more critical the task, the more signoffs needed.

Consider the following guidelines for placing signoffs in procedures:

1. Proper use of signoffs will decrease the probability of error, but overuse of signoffs has little effect, positive or negative, on procedure performance.

2. Some organizations require a signoff at each step in certain categories of critical procedures, such as main-

tenance or testing of safety-related equipment. A test procedure in which a slight confusion between two pushbuttons could cause the plant to shut down is a good example. However, most types of procedures should have signoffs only at important steps.

3. The procedure should provide adequate space for the signoff, and it should be clear to the user what type of signoff is required.
4. If signoffs are to be listed on an attachment such as a data sheet, the procedure step should refer the user to the appropriate part of the data sheet each time a signoff is required. It is not sufficient to merely provide space for the signoff on the data sheet without supporting instruction in the procedure.
5. If a signoff is required for a step that may be optional or not applicable under all conditions, the procedure step should instruct the user to mark the signoff "N/A" if the step is not to be done.
6. If there are special conditions or methods for verification before signing off, these should be stated. For example, an independent verifier other than the procedure user is to verify that a valve is left in the fully closed position. This fact can be verified by observing the remote indication in the control room. If, however, the procedural task requires actual observation of the valve itself, the procedure should state that verification must take place at the valve and that observing a remote indicator is not sufficient verification.
7. When a series of steps requiring signoffs may need to be repeated several times, such as a calibration task, a signoff at the end of the series is preferable to individual step signoffs to avoid unnecessary documentation and possible confusion. However, if you know that the same sequence must be done two times, for example, for redundant equipment, two different departments, or the

like, then you should provide two columns of signoffs clearly labeled as to their use.

Hold Points. A hold point is a type of verification where work must literally stop until another person, such as an inspector or supervisor, witnesses or verifies the correctness of performance. That person then usually completes a signoff before work resumes. A hold point can be formatted separately from a step, as in the following example:

HOLD: Notify Quality Control to witness the next step.

Or, the hold may be stated in a previous step:

Contact Quality Control to observe the disassembly in the next step.

A signoff for a hold point can be placed directly at the step or at the corresponding point on a data sheet. In some cases, however, where an inspector must observe an entire sequence of steps or is required several times in a procedure, one final signoff that all verifications were performed may be sufficient.

2.7.9 Planning the Need for Referencing and Branching

While developing your expanded outline, you may determine that the user will need information or must follow a task sequence that is already in another procedure. Or, you may determine that the user will need to jump forward or backward in the step sequence or perhaps completely out of the procedure. These situations require you to consider proper use of referencing and branching.

- **Referencing** is defined as sending the user to another procedure or to another step or section in the same procedure, but expecting the user to return to where he/she left off.
- **Branching** is defined as sending the user to another procedure or to another step or section in the same procedure also, but the user is *not* expected to return to where he/she left off. In the course of branching, the

user may skip steps entirely and never perform them. The work conditions determine what steps he/she performs.

Some referencing and branching cannot be avoided. However, you should be aware that performance problems and errors can be caused by overuse of referencing and branching. Indeed, a common procedure user complaint is "too much referencing."

Referencing. Performance problems related to referencing are:

- The user loses track of where he/she left off.
- The user overlooks important prerequisites, precautions, cautions, or notes preceding the step to which he/she is referenced.
- The user has problems handling the multiple procedures needed to perform one task, or has no workspace to lay them out.
- Because of the nuisance factor of referencing, the user may tend to rely on memory rather than retrieve the referenced procedure(s).

When you determine that referencing may be required, consider the following guidelines in your decision:

1. Consider the length of the material you need to reference. Do not send a user out of the current sequence for the sake of two or three steps that are elsewhere. Repeat those steps in the current sequence. However, if you need to reference the user to another procedure for lengthy instructions on how to complete a form, for example, do so rather than repeating those instructions in your procedure and making it unnecessarily bulky.
2. If you decide to repeat information in your procedure, be sure to include your source in the References section of your procedure. A recurring problem in organizations is the ripple effect of revision in one procedure. If your References section is complete, then it will be clear that revision of the procedure listed may affect your procedure.

3. Even if you do not repeat the information but simply reference the other procedure, you should be sure to include that procedure in your References section. Any procedure or document you mention in your procedure text should be in your References section.
4. If important precautionary information precedes the referenced step or section, consider referencing the user directly to that information first. Some organizations handle this matter by training their personnel to always review the prerequisites and precautions of any procedure to which they are referenced. However, in a critical task, an extra reminder would be in order.
5. Ensure that it is clear to the user where he/she must return after completing the referenced instruction. Some referencing instructions are obvious. For example, "Document value on Data Sheet 1" is a sufficient referencing instruction. It would not be necessary to add "and return to this step."
6. Avoid unnecessary forward or backward referencing. One procedure asked the user, who was in Step 3, to refer to a diagram in Step 7 for some needed information to perform Step 3. A better placement of the diagram would have been at Step 3, where it was first mentioned. Then, to avoid a backward reference, the writer might have chosen to repeat the diagram at Step 7. You will need to judge whether you should repeat information or use a backward reference based on how much "page flipping" would be required of the user.
7. If the procedure involves reassembly of an item that was disassembled earlier in the procedure, *DO NOT* reference the user to the disassembly steps and instruct that they be performed in reverse order. If any backward reference will cause an error, it is this one. You should supply complete reassembly instructions in the procedure. In fact, to be sure they are consistent with the disassembly steps, outline the two tasks at the same time.

In Chapter 3, Drafting the Procedure, we will discuss how referencing statements should be worded, and the specific verbs that should be used.

Branching. Performance problems related to branching are:

- The user must work through a series of several procedures to accomplish a task.
- The user becomes confused when too much branching causes him/her to lose track of the work progress.
- The user becomes trapped in an endless loop because there are no criteria for getting out or because he/she cannot meet the criteria for getting out.

Consider the following guidelines for branching:

- If a user is branched forward, skipping over some steps, ensure that you give instructions to N/A the skipped steps if required by your organization's policy.
- Use appropriate wording and action verbs (to be discussed in Chapter 3) to ensure that the user understands the instruction is a branch (meaning he/she does not have to return) and not a reference.
- As was discussed above under "Signoffs," consider the need for multiple signoffs for a series of steps to which the user must branch more than once. Either provide multiple columns of signoffs or provide one signoff at the conclusion of the series.

In Chapter 3, Drafting Stage, we will discuss the appropriate wording and action verbs that you should use in branching instructions.

2.7.10 Planning Figures, Tables, Data Sheets, and Checklists

As you analyze and organize information and develop the expanded outline, the need for graphics, that is, nontext items such as figures (including graphs, diagrams, drawings, and other illustrations), tables, data sheets, and checklists, will become apparent. The types of graphics needed will depend on your analysis of the technical and user information. These graphics should serve as aids to the user in performing the procedural tasks.

When developing graphics, consider the guidelines discussed below. Chapter 3 contains specific information on designing and formatting different types of graphics.

General Guidelines. On the basis of the user and technical information you have analyzed, determine:

- Whether graphics are needed
- The type of graphic that would serve the user the best
- Where the graphics should be placed
- What support services are needed to produce the graphics

Tables and Graphs. Tables organize information and help the user obtain and use data. Graphs present a visual image of the relationship of data. Both tables and graphs can help reduce the need for the user to make interpretations of data obtained while performing the task. An example is providing a table of possible values instead of requiring the user to calculate values with a formula. Reducing the need for interpretation also reduces the probability of error. Consider using a table or graph whenever the user will need to analyze obtained data, such as determine trends or compare measurements with acceptable or desired values.

Diagrams, Drawings, and Illustrations. The types of illustrations included in a procedure contribute to its usability. The illustrations used in a procedure should *help* the user. Including illustrations that are not usable, such as a figure from a vendor's manual that has been reduced so much the information cannot be read, only serves to frustrate the user and add to the difficulty of performing the procedure. Consider illustrations that help the user locate items that are infrequently used, have poor access, or are not labeled.

Flowcharts. A flowchart is used to summarize the process described in the procedure. A flowchart serves as an excellent planning tool (an alternative to an outline of the steps) you can develop before drafting the procedure, because it shows an overview of the task sequence. Then the flowchart may be useful as an attachment to the final procedure.

Data Sheets and Checklists. Data sheets and checklists generally have two types of users: the procedure user who records information and the post-task reviewer who evaluates the recorded data. Data sheets and checklists should be separate from the procedure text, which should fully explain their use.

2.8 EVALUATING THE PLANNING PRODUCT

At this point you should have completed your expanded outline, having taken into consideration the guidance presented above. The last step in planning is to evaluate the expanded outline. Evaluating the expanded outline will identify any information gaps in the procedure, and will serve as an objective review of the procedure's completeness and technical accuracy.

Several people can evaluate your expanded outline, preferably at the same time. You should be sure to indicate the date/time that you need the outline returned. You should also be as specific as possible as to what you would like each evaluator to look for. For example, you may have concerns about whether information was omitted, and you ask a subject matter expert to look for "holes" in the process or task described.

Potential evaluators include:

- **Peer**. A peer in your working group may not have detailed technical knowledge of the procedure content, although he/she probably has a technical background similar to yours. See if the peer can follow the sequence described.
- **User**. Having a potential user review the planning product is an excellent method of obtaining an early field test. If possible, select a less experienced user.

- **Supervisor**. Having your supervisor review your planning product can save time in the review stage. In general, it can be said that the more time you invest in planning, the less time you will need in the review stage, prarticularly the formal review and approval process. The supervisor gets an early opportunity to comment on the outline and request clarification where needed. Thus, you obtain his/her comments and reactions before you invest heavily in drafting. How many times have you fully drafted a document, only to have a supervisor say "That's not what I had in mind"? You can avoid this situation if you give the supervisor the chance to make his/her expectations clearly before you start to draft. In the end, it may save you a great deal of revision and rewrite time.

Once you have received comments from your evaluator(s), review them and revise your outline as you think appropriate. This revised outline will be your guide or "roadmap" for drafting and will also be one of the criteria against which you will review your draft in the review stage.

3

Drafting the Procedure

You should be approaching the drafting stage with a nearly complete procedure, that is, an expanded outline that includes:

- Noninstructional sections, such as Purpose or References, developed fully
- An outline or flowchart of the procedure steps
- Preliminary graphics, such as figures, tables, and forms

If you had others evaluate this expanded outline, you should have resolved any comments and revised the outline accordingly.

Our major goals in drafting are to:

- Provide technically accurate information
- Use the appropriate and correct format according to industry or corporate requirements and guidelines
- Make the procedure readable and easy to use by expressing ideas clearly and concisely
- Be consistent in format and writing style
- Build in flexibility where appropriate so that the user can adjust the procedure task to varying conditions

If we can meet all the above, the user will be able to perform the procedure efficiently and correctly.

3.1 CHAPTER OBJECTIVES

At the conclusion of this chapter, you should be able to:

3.1 Select an appropriate text/graphics format based on the procedure's purpose.

3.2 Describe a recommended step numbering system.

3.3 Describe minimum recommended page identificaton information.

3.4 Construct a deductive paragraph.

3.5 Apply action step construction guidelines.

3.6 Develop the following steps in the appropriate format:
- Conditional statements
- Steps with multiple objects of action verbs

3.7 Use parallel structure in procedure development.

3.8 State the purpose and guidelines for format and placement of cautions and notes.

3.9 Use appropriate wording for referencing and branching.

3.10 Select appropriate words for procedure steps: verbs and vocabulary.

3.11 Use specific equipment nomenclature in proper format.

3.12 Apply guidelines for using acronyms and abbreviations.

3.13 Develop appropriate acceptance criteria and tolerances.

3.14 Apply rules of spelling, capitalization, methods of emphasis, and punctuation.

3.15 Use numerical values properly.

3.16 Discuss criteria for effective procedure graphics.

3.17 Name sources of graphics.

3.18 State techniques to enhance graphics.

3.2 HUMAN FACTORS IN DRAFTING

Some of the human factors considerations discussed in Chapter 2 are particularly applicable to the drafting stage:

- **Procedure Format**. A user expects to find information located in specific sections and presented in a consistent manner. If information can be found readily and the format is used consistently, readability improves and the probability of error decreases.
- **Level of Detail**. The appropriate level of detail results from the writer considering the user, the task, and the environment during the planning stage, and then providing enough detail for the least qualified user to perform the task during the drafting stage. As each step is fully drafted, the writer must select the writing style and vocabulary to achieve the appropriate detail.
- **Concept Load and Concept Density**. A procedure writer must consider these variables when drafting the steps in a procedure because each instruction must be as simple and concise as possible to minimize the concept load and density the user is asked to comprehend. Paragraph-style instructions are discouraged specifically because of this variable.
- **Document Design**. Chapter 2 discussed document design features as a method of focusing the user's attention on the organization of ideas in the procedure. During the drafting stage, the writer considers document design features such as indenting instructions to show main ideas and related details, using space clues such as vertical format for multiple objects of an action verb, and highlighting important information with methods of emphasis such as full capital letters and underlining.
- **Writing Style and Language**. For the fewest errors in using written procedures, the writing style should place minimal demands on the user. In the drafting stage, the choice of language, both sentence structure and vocabulary, is constantly made with the user in mind. Although the procedure writer may be an engineer with the

appropriate higher degrees, the user may be a technician with a high school education. The language must be chosen so that the user can comprehend it easily and perform the instruction accurately.

3.3 APPROACH TO DRAFTING PRINCIPLES

This chapter approaches drafting deductively; that is, we start with general, global principles concerning the overall document and work our way down to specific principles such as word choice. We then conclude with guidance on procedure graphics. The major topics are:

- Procedure Format
- Document Design
- Effective Paragraphs
- Action Step Construction
- Word Choice
- Mechanics of Style
- Procedure Graphics
- Drafting Stage: The Final Product

3.4 PROCEDURE FORMAT

Procedure format as discussed here refers to the procedure's physical layout on the page. Three basic page layouts are used for procedures: single-column, multicolumn, and flowchart. Your company policy most likely dictates the required page layout for procedures. However, each format has advantages and disadvantages in use, and may be more appropriate in one environment than in another.

Another variable in page layout is the placement of graphics, which also has advantages and disadvantages. Ways to place graphics in procedures will be discussed below along with the basic page layouts.

3.4.1 Single-Column Format

The single-column format is the most common format used in written procedures. In this format, the procedure uses standard left and right margins. This format can accommodate any type of procedure content, but it lends itself best to describing a linear process rather than a process where two or more tasks must be performed concurrently by multiple personnel. This format also allows the most space on a page to describe procedure steps, as opposed to a multicolumn format where the horizontal space in each column is vastly reduced, or a flowchart format where space is limited to the area within the various flowchart symbols. Figure 3-1 shows a typical technical procedure page in a single-column format.

Four methods of positioning graphics in single-column procedures are: attached, integrated, combination of attached and integrated, and facing page. Each is described below.

Attached Graphics. Attaching graphics at the end of a procedure is the most common method of positioning graphics in both single- and multicolumn procedures. This method is the easiest for the writer, the word processing personnel, and the photocopying personnel, but it is inconvenient for the user, who must flip back and forth between pages. In fact, the environment in which the procedure is to be used may preclude this method of attached graphics altogether because of the criticality, speed, or difficulty of the task.

However, attaching graphics at the end of a procedure is the best method in two situations:

- When the graphic is a full page in size
- When the graphic is referenced more than once in the procedure

Figure 3-2 is an example of a graphic formatted as an attachment.

IC-2-161.06
Rev. 4
Page 11 of 15

10.6.9 Using PS1, apply inputs as required by Attachment 2. Record the outputs in the As Found column for Tests 2 and 3.

10.6.10 If As Found readings for Tests 1, 2, and 3 are within tolerance, go to Step 10.6.22.
If NOT within tolerance, continue with next step.

10.6.11 Position Switch 1 to the "GROUND" position.

10.6.12 Adjust "BAL" adjustment for 0.0 VDC output.

10.6.13 Repeat Tests 1, 2, and 3. Record output on Attachment 1.

10.6.14 Position Switch 1 to the "GROUND" position.

10.6.15 Adjust PS1 for +10.0 VDC.

10.6.16 Position to TC knob to the 10-sec position.

10.6.17 Position Switch 1 to the PS1 position. Verify the LAG unit output decreases as follows:

- To -6.32 VDC in 10 sec (9-11 sec)
- To -8.65 VDC in 20 sec (18-22 sec)
- To -9.5 VDC in 30 sec (27-33 sec)
- To -9.8 VDC in 40 sec (36-44 sec)
- To -9.9 VDC in 50 sec (45-55 sec)

If the LAG unit output follows this characteristic, indicate YES on Attachment 2.

10.6.18 Position Switch 1 to the "GROUND" position.

10.6.19 Adjust PS1 for -10.0 VDC.

10.6.20 Repeat Step 10.6.17 for an increasing output.

10.6.21 Repeat Steps 10.6.11 through 10.6.20 until required results are obtained.
If required results are NOT obtained, notify supervisor.

10.6.22 Record As Left readings on Attachment 2.

10.6.23 Return TC knob to the As Found position and record this setting in As Left column on Attachment 2.

Figure 3-1. Example of Single-Column Format

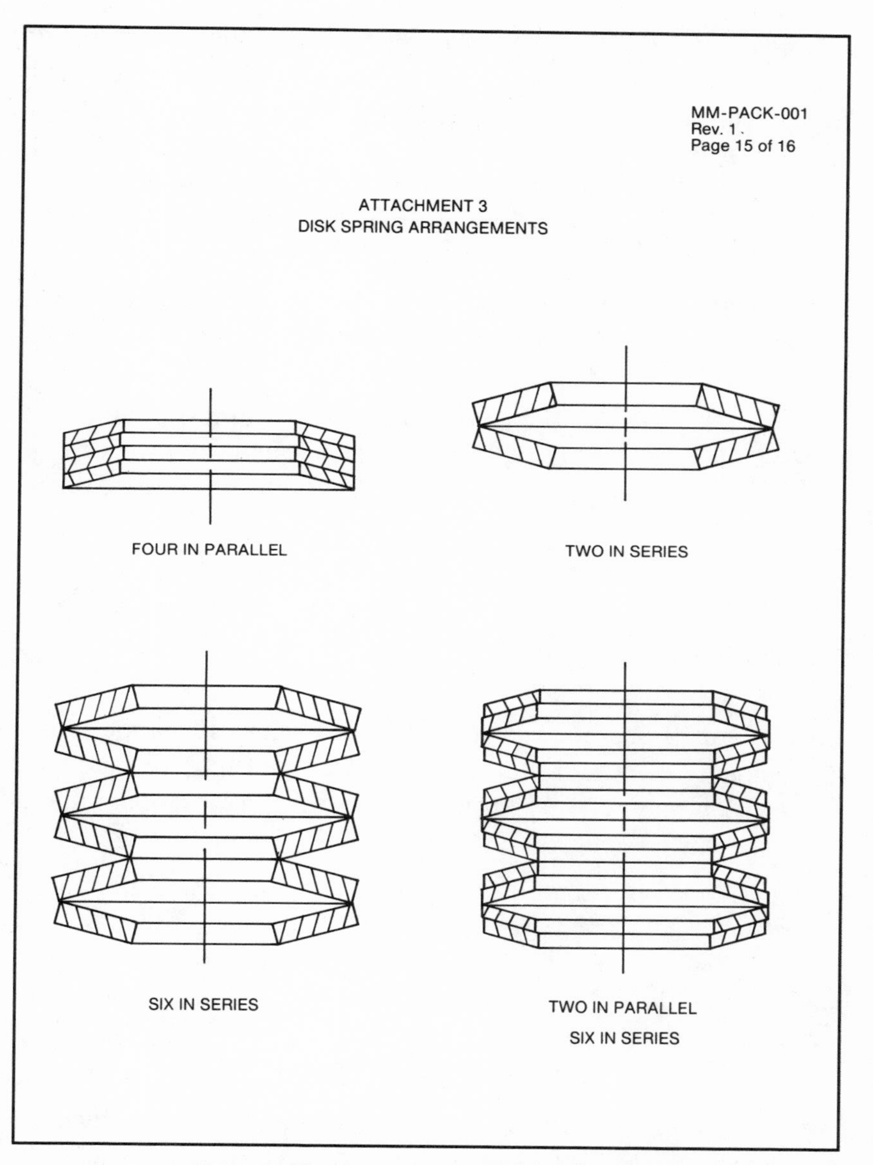

Figure 3-2. Example of Attached Graphics

Integrated Graphics. When graphics are integrated with the procedure steps, we achieve the best association between text and graphics. This method eliminates flipping back and forth between text and attachments. The figure or table immediately follows the step that mentions it. When a graphic is needed more than once, it must be repeated after each step that mentions it.

- The writer must measure the space needed for each graphic and instruct word processing personnel to leave spaces where required.
- Word processing personnel must leave the required spaces on the initial draft and succeeding revisions, which may require "juggling" of text to accommodate the graphics.

The disadvantages of this method are:

- The writer must measure the space needed for each graphic and instruct word processing personnel to leave spaces where required.
- Word processing personnel must leave the required spaces on the initial draft and succeeding revisions, which may require "juggling" of text to accommodate the graphics.

Figure 3-3 is an example of a procedure page with an integrated graphic.

Combination of Attached and Integrated Graphics. This method combines the first two, and graphics are placed depending on the following criteria:

- If a graphic is a full page in size, it is attached.
- If a graphic is a data sheet, form, or checklist, it is attached.
- If the graphic is less than a full page, it is placed following the step where it is needed. If it is needed again in the procedure, it is repeated after the appropriate step.

MP-160-002
Rev. 9
Page 17 of 60

5.16.23 Slowly release the hydraulic pressure. Unscrew the puller bars.

5.16.24 Move the tensioners to the next studs indicated in the diagram below:

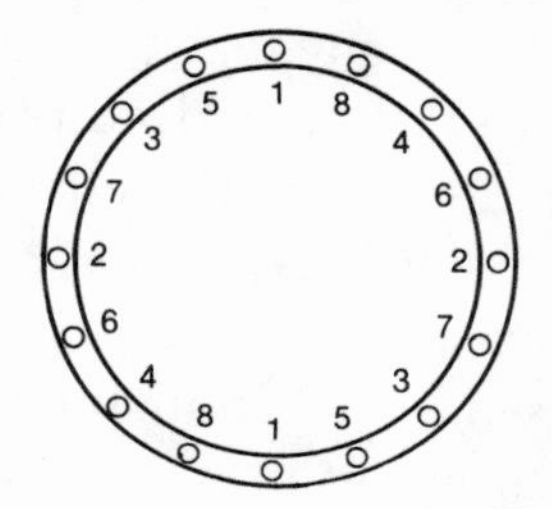

5.16.25 Repeat Steps 5.16.21 through 5.16.24 until all the stud nuts are tightened.

5.16.26 Complete Steps 5.16.21 through 5.16.24 for all stud nuts using 7600 psig hydraulic pressure.

5.16.27 Complete Steps 5.16.21 through 5.16.24 for all stud nuts using 9500 psig hydraulic pressure.

5.16.28 Install the pump motor per Section 5.13 of this procedure.

5.16.29 Connect the seal and the seal cooling piping.

5.17 Torque Procedure

5.17.1 Clean all nuts and bolts. Visually inspect the threads for nicks and burrs.

5.17.2 Lubricate all stainless nuts and bolts with Grade SS lubricant.

5.17.3 Lubricate all carbon steel nuts and bolts with Grade OS lubricant.

5.17.4 Follow the bolt tightening sequence shown in the diagram below:

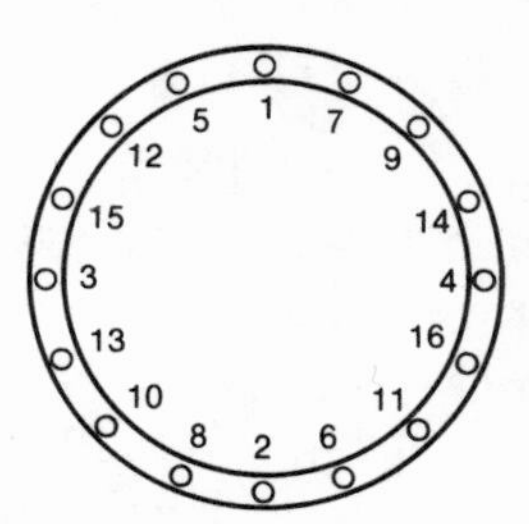

Figure 3-3. Example of Integrated Graphics

- If the graphic is less than a full page, but it is referenced several times so that repeating it each time would unnecessarily lengthen the procedure, then it is attached.

Facing Page Graphics. If the graphic is a figure or table, it is placed on the left-hand page facing the procedure text to which it applies. If the graphic is a data sheet, form, or checklist that must be filled in by the user, it should be placed on the right-hand page, with the procedure text on the left-hand page.

This method is very helpful for the user, who does not have to flip back and forth between text and graphics. However, you should ensure that the work environment allows the user to comfortably use a procedure that must be opened and laid out like a book.

The disadvantages of this method are:

- The procedure may be longer because only those steps that relate to a graphic may be placed on the page opposite that graphic.
- The procedure requires more care in word processing, proofreading, and photocopying because of the double-sided format.

Figure 3-4 illustrates the facing page format.

3.4.2 Multicolumn Format

A multicolumn format is any format that uses at least two columns of text or graphics on each page. Many variations are used in corporate and industrial procedures.

Double-Column Format. The most common multicolumn format is the double-column format. This format is used for the instructional section of the procedure. The two columns are used in several different ways:

- The first column is used for action steps, and the second for any or all of the following:

  Contingency Actions (what to do if the stated action cannot be performed or if the expected plant response is not obtained)

  - Details (substeps for the higher level step stated in the first column)
  - Notes (helpful or supplemental information, such as a valve name where only the number has been stated in the first column, or the location of a component named in the step)
  - Rationale (the reason for accomplishing the step)
  - Comments (a column title that can be used to cover all the uses stated above)
- The first column is used to name the person (by functional title) responsible for the action given in the second column. Column titles commonly used are "Who" and "What."
- The first column is used for action steps, and the second column for a figure related to these steps. (The procedure page would have to be oriented horizontally rather than vertically for this format.)

Figure 3-5 illustrates several types of double-column procedures.

Other Multicolumn Formats. Some organizations use three columns within their procedures. As with the double-column procedures, this format begins with the action step portion of the procedure.

Many different multicolumn formats can be designed depending on the type of task. Here are some examples:

- For a diagnostic or troubleshooting procedure:
  - Column 1: Symptom
  - Column 2: Action
  - Column 3: Verification (indicates system response so that user can determine whether the action was successful)

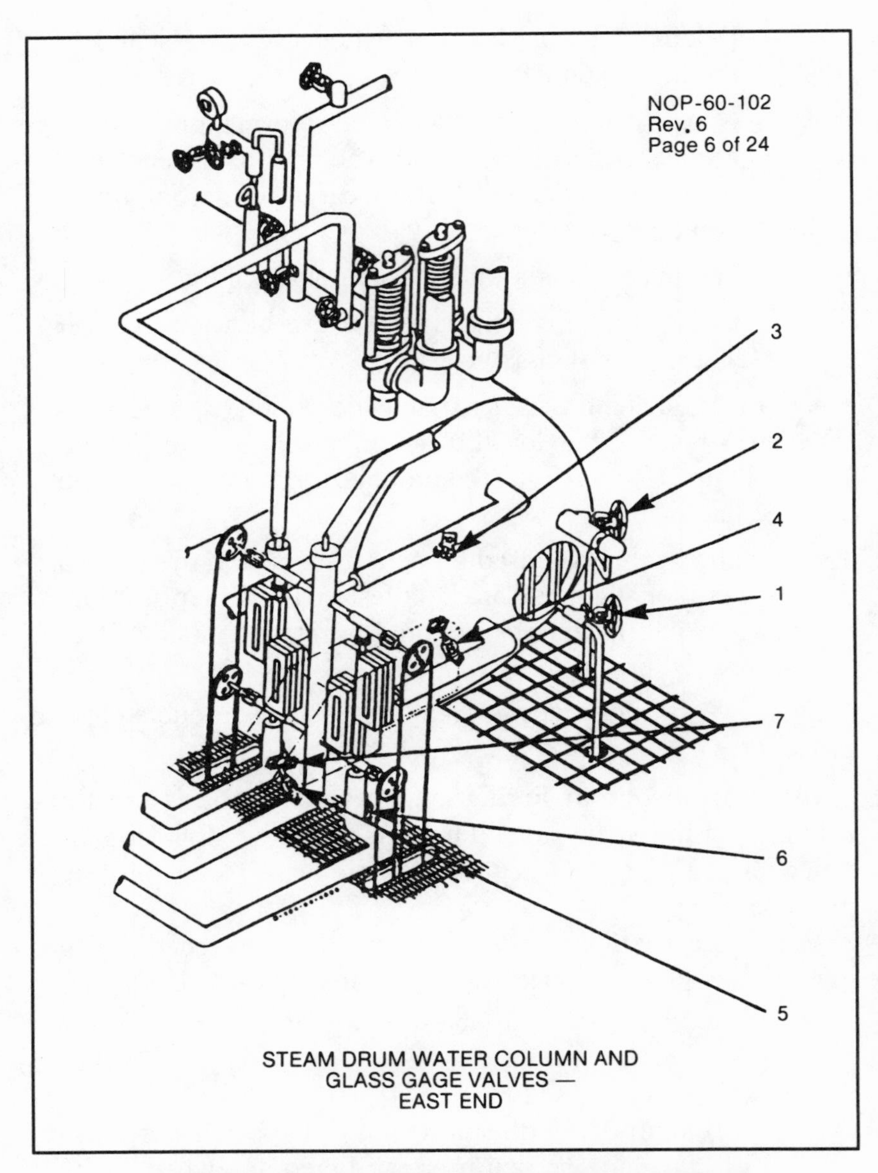

Figure 3-4. Example of Facing Page Format

NOP-60-102
Rev. 6
Page 7 of 24

3.3 Valving at Top of Boiler (continued)

3.3.1 Open the following valves:

a. Instrumentation block valve HPV-606 (1).
b. Instrumentation block valve HPV-607 (2).
c. Steam-side water column block valve (3).
d. Water-side water column block valve (4).
e. Water column drain valve (5).
f. Bi-color gage drain valve (6).
g. Clear gage drain valve (7).

Figure 3-4. Example of Facing Page Format (continued)

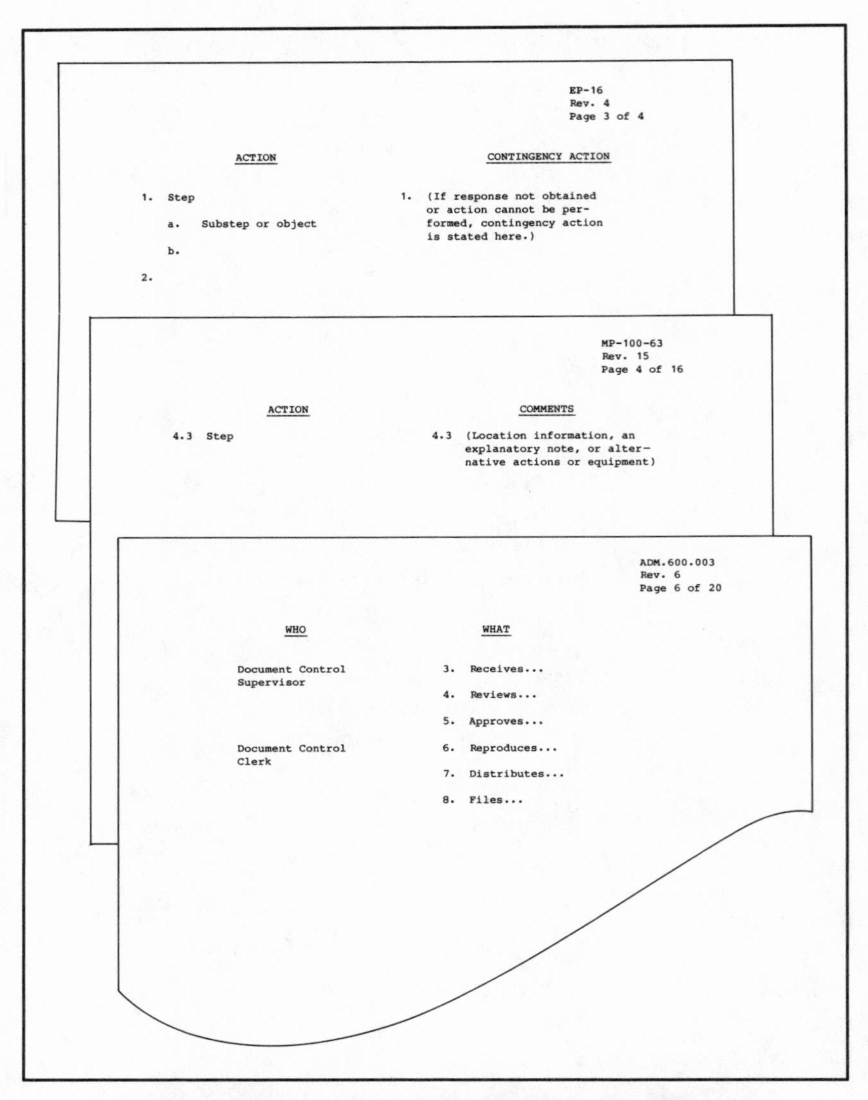

Figure 3-5. Examples of Double-Column Formats

- For a procedure involving several different personnel:
  - Column 1: Who
  - Column 2: What
  - Column 3: Notes

Figure 3-6 shows the page layouts of procedures that use three columns.

Disadvantages of Multicolumn Procedures. The major disadvantages of multicolumn procedures are:

- The writer has little space in which to write the action step, and must be very brief and succinct to avoid having a lengthy procedure. A fine level of detail cannot be accomplished in this format.
- The word processing personnel must take special care to align the appropriate material horizontally across all columns. Then, the procedure writer must ensure that the material is aligned properly when editing and proofreading the typed copy.

Graphics in Multicolumn Procedures. A multicolumn page may or may not have vertical lines separating the columns. These lines are not needed as long as there is sufficient white space between the columns. However, some organizations do use vertical lines, which permit slightly wider columns. These vertical lines are generally part of a printed, standard form used for procedure pages because many word processing systems cannot create vertical lines.

The use of vertical lines affects the positioning of graphics in a multicolumn procedure. Graphics would have to be attached to the end of the procedure, except for any small table that could be typed within a column. If vertical lines are not used, graphics could be integrated with the steps when they are less than a full page and not needed frequently throughout the procedure, as discussed above for single-column procedures.

The facing page graphics format is not suitable for multicolumn procedures because the user already has to read multiple columns

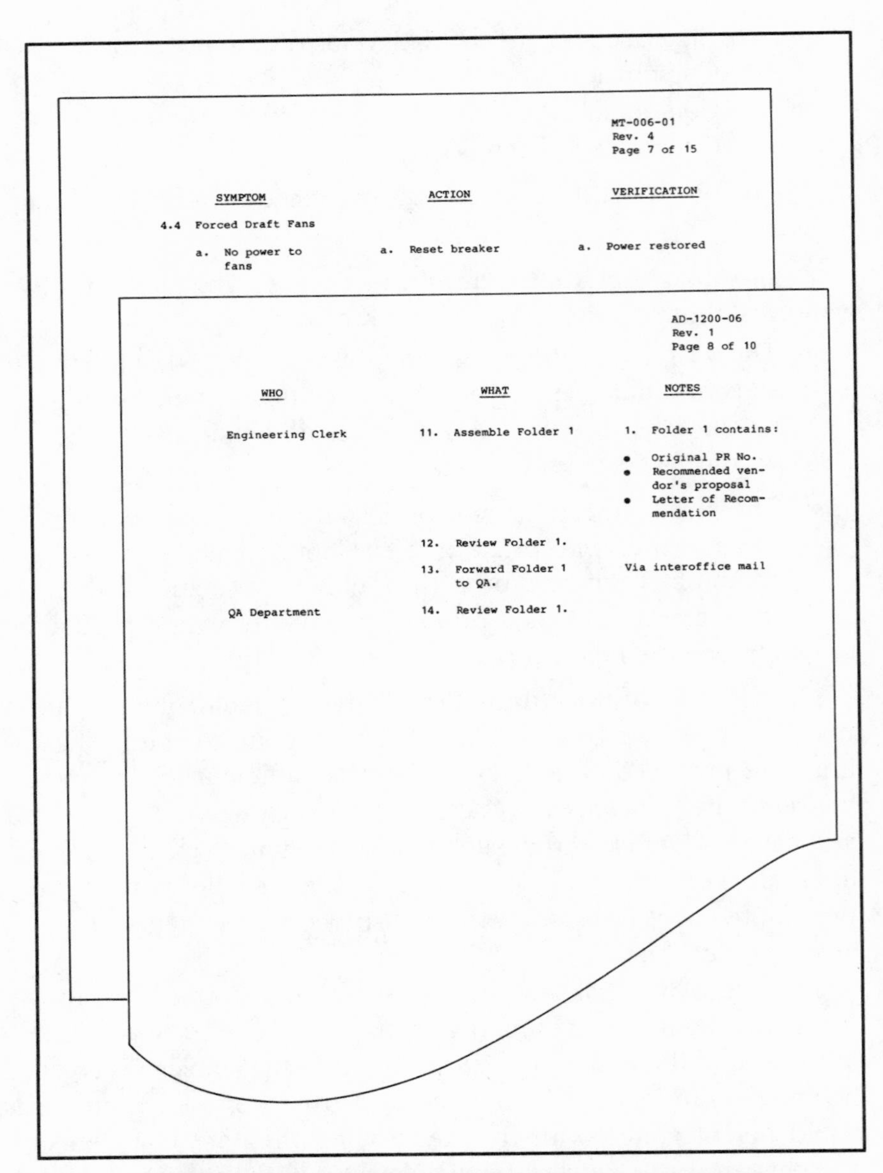

MT-006-01
Rev. 4
Page 7 of 15

SYMPTOM	ACTION	VERIFICATION
4.4 Forced Draft Fans		
a. No power to fans	a. Reset breaker	a. Power restored

AD-1200-06
Rev. 1
Page 8 of 10

WHO	WHAT	NOTES
Engineering Clerk	11. Assemble Folder 1	1. Folder 1 contains: • Original PR No. • Recommended vendor's proposal • Letter of Recommendation
	12. Review Folder 1.	
	13. Forward Folder 1 to QA.	Via interoffice mail
QA Department	14. Review Folder 1.	

Figure 3-6. Examples of Three-Column Formats

on the page, and a graphic on a facing page adds essentially another column that must be referred to. The result may be confusion for the user as to what to read first.

3.4.3 Flowchart Format

Flowchart-style procedures are currently growing in popularity because of the old adage, "A picture is worth a thousand words." The action steps of the task or process are presented in a flowchart rather than in a conventional prose format.

Uses for Flowchart Procedures. Flowchart procedures are especially suited to:

- Tasks that require many user decisions and different action step sequences based on those decisions.
- Complex processes involving multiple concurrent paths.
- Emergency or other critical procedures where the user does not have the time to read through lengthy prose procedures.

Disadvantages of Flowchart Procedures. A disadvantage of flowchart procedures is that only minimal detail can be presented within the chart symbols. In the nuclear industry, where many plants use flowcharts for their emergency operating procedures, control room operators are thoroughly trained on the procedures to eliminate the need for fine detail. In a procedure where more detail is required, a flowchart can support prose action steps as a summary of the task or process. This use of a flowchart as a supporting graphic is discussed later in this chapter under "Procedure Graphics."

Another disadvantage of flowcharts is the additional effort required to produce them. They must either be drawn by graphic artists or by a computer-aided design (CAD) system. In either case, the original creation of the charts and succeeding corrections and revisions are time consuming and expensive particularly if the charts are in an oversize format.

Flowchart Sizes. Flowchart procedures are generally sized in one of two ways:

- Standard, 8-1/2″ x 11″ page·format
- Oversize format according to any of the standard drawing sizes used for blueprints, piping and instrument drawings, and the like:
  - Size B = 11″ x 17″
  - Size C = 17″ x 22″
  - Size D = 22″ x 34″
  - Size E = 34″ x 44″
  - Size F = 28″ x 40″

  Note: Size A is the 8-1/2″ x 11″ page size.

The size chosen depends on the expected length and complexity of the chart. Obviously, an 8-1/2″ x 11″ page would not accommodate a very large chart that would still be readable. A special consideration is the width of the chart. If multiple concurrent paths must be illustrated, they must be aligned horizontally to indicate concurrent performance, and a wider horizontal dimension would be required.

The writer must also consider the environment in which the procedure will be used. An 8-1/2″ x 11″ chart could be used in any environment, whereas an oversize chart is not very portable. Oversize charts are currently in use in power plant control rooms, where one operator reads the steps to other operators who perform them. The chart remains on a table or countertop, so portability is not a problem.

Graphics in Flowchart Procedures. Graphics should be positioned in flowchart procedures according to the following criteria:

- If a small table or figure relates to one step or series of steps on the chart, place it adjacent to the first step that mentions it. If the graphic is needed again on another page, repeat it next to the appropriate step.

- If the graphic is a large figure or table or is anything that must be filled in by the user, such as a checklist or data sheet, format it as an attachment to the procedure. If the flowcharts themselves are oversize, the 8-1/2″ x 11″ attachments should be filed separately, and the user should be trained to know where to locate these attachments.

Flowchart Examples. Figure 3-7 lists symbols typically used in procedure flowcharts. An organization may of course use variations of these symbols or different symbols altogether in its own procedures. Figures 3-8 and 3-9 are examples of an 8-1/2″ x 11″ flowchart and an oversize flowchart. The oversize chart also illustrates positioning of graphics on a chart.

3.5 DOCUMENT DESIGN

Document design refers to certain format elements, such as step numbering, that must be considered to enhance a procedure's readability. The way the printed word is arranged on the page can improve or hinder a reader's comprehension. It affects the rate at which the words are read and understood. A reader will read and understand a series of lengthy, closely spaced paragraphs at a much slower rate than a list of numbered, short sentences with a double space between them. Horizontal "space clues" also help the reader. Indentation of subordinate items is a space clue that tells the reader the material consists of details supporting the main idea.

Document design also concerns procedure identification and numbering. A procedure needs a cover page that identifies it completely for the user and also tells the user whether it is the correct or latest revision. If a procedure does not have a cover page, then complete identification information must be on the first page. The procedure number and title must be unique to distinguish the procedure from similar ones in the same facility. Most procedure designation systems use combinations of letters and numbers so that the user can tell, for example, the procedure category or the major system it covers.

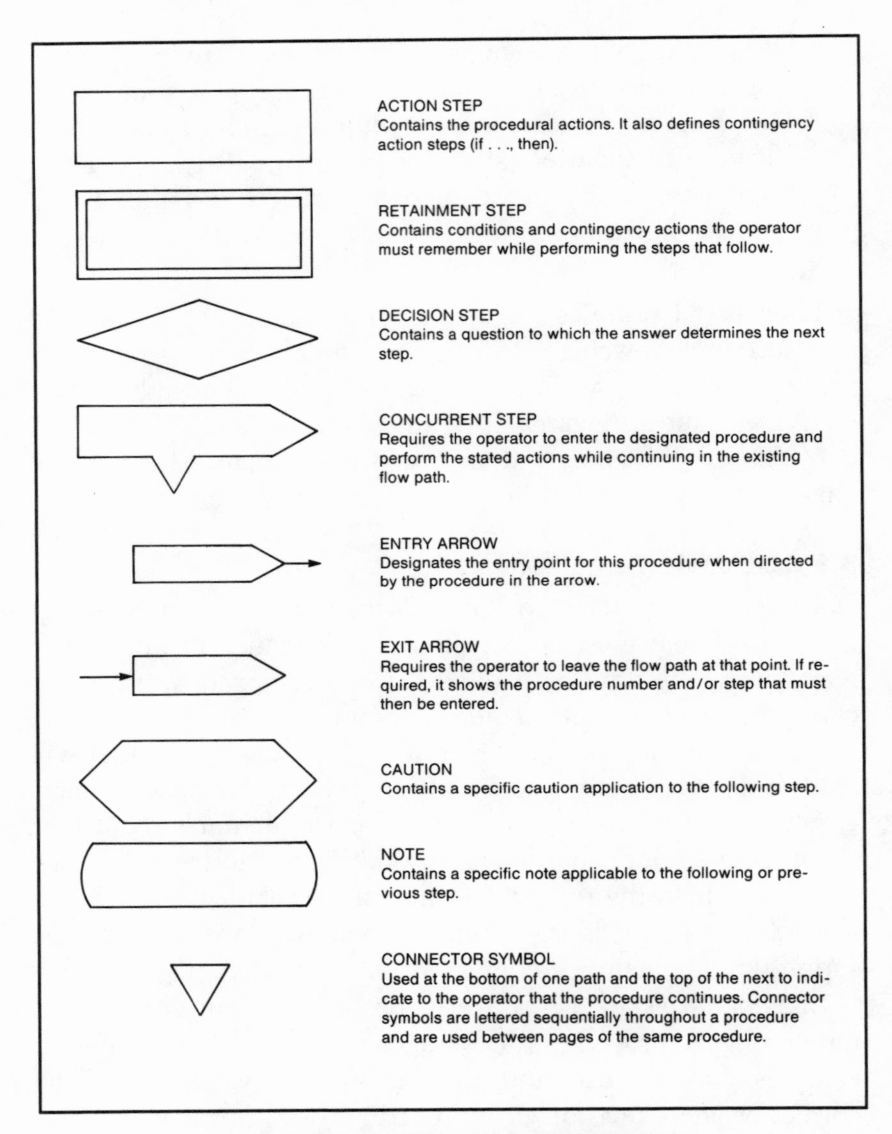

Figure 3-7. Flowchart Symbols

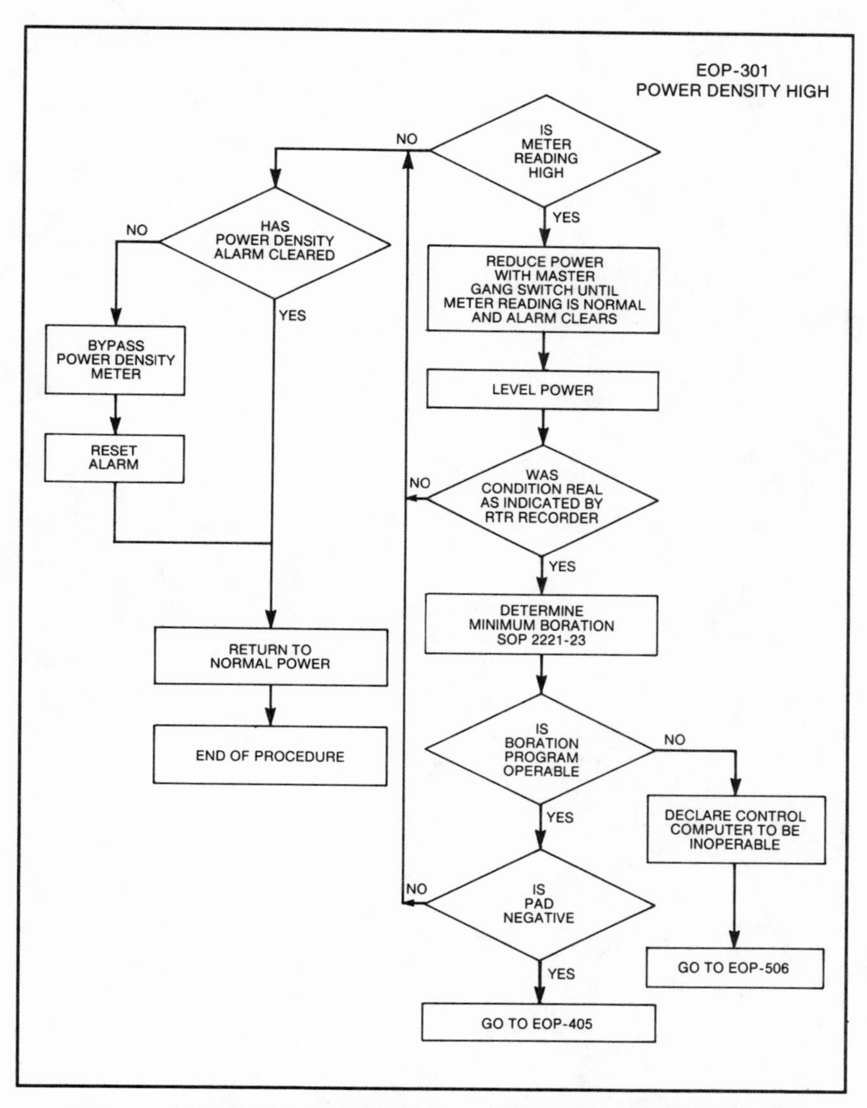

Figure 3-8. Sample 8-1/2" x 11" Flowchart Procedure

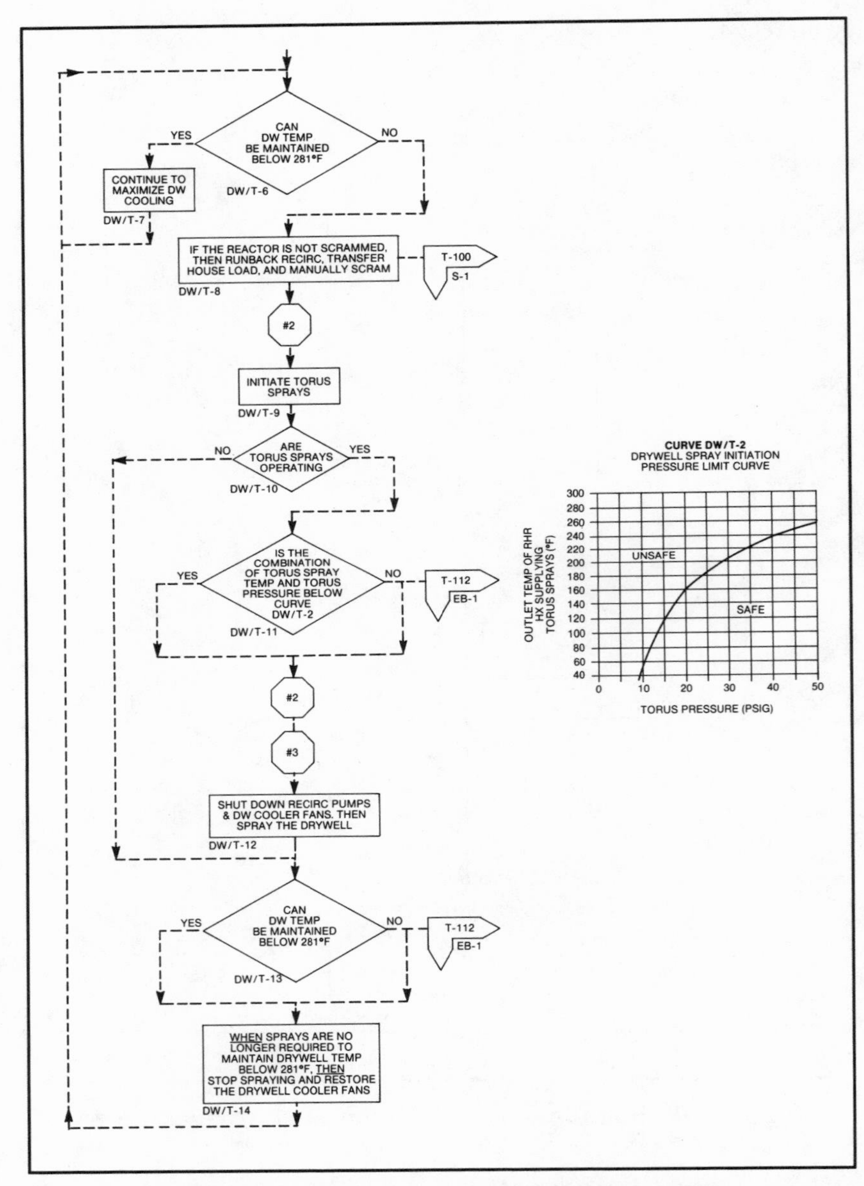

Figure 3-9. Segment of an Oversize Flowchart Procedure

A third area of document design is page numbering and identification. Each page of a procedure should be completely identified and numbered.

A final document design consideration is the breakdown of topics or major sections in a procedure. No matter the type of procedure, it should be presented in logical sections.

These four areas of document design—numbering and identification of procedure steps, or step hierarchy; procedure identification and numbering; page identification and numbering; and breakdown of major sections—are discussed in detail below.

3.5.1 Step Hierarchy

A procedure's purpose is to give instructions on how to perform a task. The instructions, or steps, should be numbered and arranged for maximum reader comprehension and, therefore, efficient task performance.

Many step numbering systems exist, but all systems should incorporate indentation of subtopics. Here are some examples:

Example 1: Standard Outline Format

VII. PROCEDURE
    A. Task 1
        1. Step
            a. Substep or list of objects
                (a) Sub-substep or list of objects
                    (1) List of objects

Example 2: Decimal Format

7.0 PROCEDURE
    7.1 Task 1
        7.1.1 Step
            7.1.1.1 Substep or list of objects
                a. Sub-substep or list of objects
                    (1) List of objects

Example 3: Decimal Format Variation for Double-Column Procedure

ACTION	CONTINGENCY ACTION
7.0 PROCEDURE 7.1 Task 1 7.1.1 Step a. Substep (1) Sub-substep (a) List of objects	(Contingency or supporting actions use same numbering system and must align horizontally with the left-column actions to which they relate.)

Example 4: Simplified Numbering for Three-Column Procedure

SYMPTOM	ACTION	EXPECTED RESPONSE
B.	1.	1.
	2.	2.
	3.	3.

It is best to avoid numerous sublevels. Using more than four or five sublevels creates a very narrow column of text in a single-column procedure and is virtually impossible to accommodate in a multicolumn procedure, where each column is already narrow. If you find yourself repeatedly having to resort to deep indentation, consider reorganizing your topics to eliminate the problem. You may be trying to cover too many major tasks, and your procedure may need to be split into multiple ones. If you discover you have such a problem in the drafting stage, then you have not planned your procedure thoroughly. You should return to the planning stage and reorganize your information. You should then revise your planning product, the expanded outline, so that it clearly indicates the level of subordination required *before* you start to draft.

If you are developing a flowchart procedure, you will still need a simple numbering system. At a minimum, step symbols should be numbered consecutively. More complex styles are also used. See the two examples below:

Example 1: Simplified Step Numbering in a Flowchart

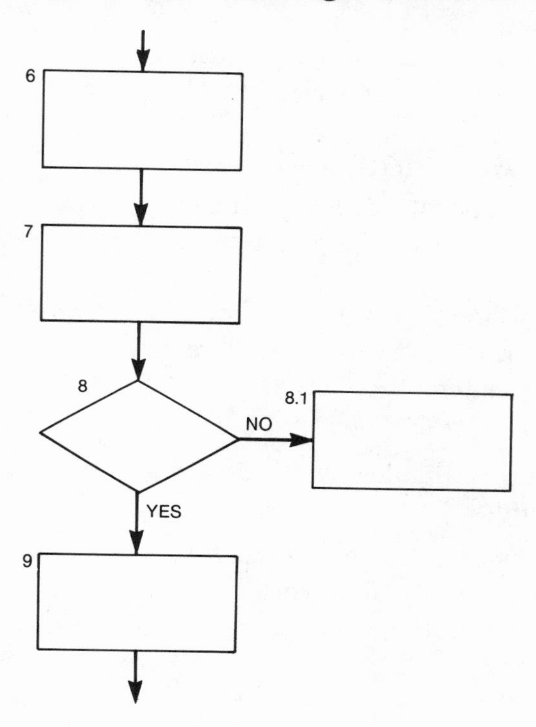

Example 2: Step Numbering with Path Identification in a Flowchart

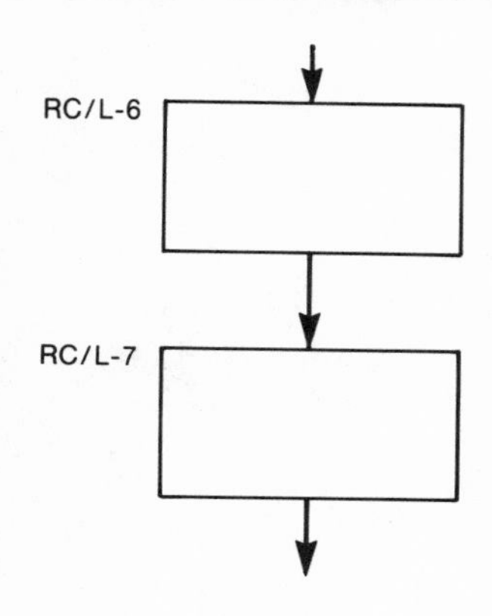

(RC/L = Reactor Control, Level path. This path deals with the reactor level within the overall procedure on reactor control.)

Step numbering is not only helpful in letting users know where they are in the procedure, it is essential where cross-referencing among steps or procedures is required. Users can be easily referred to a step when it is clearly and logically numbered.

3.5.2 Procedure Identification and Numbering

This area of document design includes the procedure title, procedure cover page (or first page), and procedure number or designator.

Procedure Title. Keep the procedure title as brief as possible, but specific enough that the procedure cannot be confused with any other procedure. In addition:

- Keep the title to 10 words or less.
- Phrase it so that key words are at or near the beginning of the title.

Some facilities keep a computerized list of procedure titles and can sort the list by the first word or two. For example, the titles of all procedures dealing with the condensate pumps would begin with "Condensate Pump." Thus, if you were tasked with revising procedures affected by a change in certain equipment, you could easily access all procedures dealing with that equipment.

Here are some examples of procedure titles:

- POOR: Functional Test of Auxiliary Boiler (nondescriptive first word)
  GOOD: Auxiliary Boiler Functional Test
- POOR: Plant Procedures (too vague)
  GOOD: Plant Procedure Writer's Guide
- POOR: Procedure for Removing Process Instrumentation from and Returning It to Service (redundant, wordy)
  GOOD: Process Instrumentation Removal from and Return to Service

Most organizations use procedure categories, such as Operating Procedures or Maintenance Procedures. The category name helps describe the procedure, so that words like "operation" or "maintenance" can be eliminated from the title. For example, "Feedwater System" would be an adequate procedure title as long as the procedure category indicates what is to be done with the system (operation, maintenance, periodic test, etc.).

Procedure Cover Page or First Page. Your facility should use a standard form or format for all procedures or at least for all procedures within a category. The cover page or first page should contain the following minimum identification information:

- Procedure number or designator
- Procedure title
- Procedure revision number or some method of indicating the procedure's currency, such as last change incorporated
- Company name
- Facility or plant name
- For power plants, the unit number if the plant has more than one unit
- A method of indicating the total number of pages in the procedure, such as:
  - A "List of Effective Pages," which lists all pages and attachments in the procedure, and may include the revision number or date or both of each page
  - A page number such as "1 of 25"

Most companies also include the signatures of the preparer, reviewer(s), and approver(s) to indicate that the procedure is approved for use.

Figure 3-10 is a sample procedure cover page. Figure 3-11 illustrates identification information on page 1 of a procedure.

Procedure Number or Designator. The procedure numbering system should be exactly that, a *system*, and should be used consistently company-wide. The procedure number may be as simple or elaborate as your company requires, but controls on

Form 24673-87

AMERICAN PETROCHEMICAL COMPANY
OPERATING PROCEDURE

Procedure No. ____________________
Revision No. ____________________

PLANT ____

PROCEDURE TITLE ____

____

PREPARER ______________________ DATE __________________

REVIEWER(S) ____________________ DATE __________________

______________________________ DATE __________________

APPROVED BY ____________________ DATE __________________

This revision incorporates changes ______________ through __________

REVISION SUMMARY (Describe nature of revision.) ______________________

____

____

____

____

____

____

____

Figure 3-10. Sample Procedure Cover Page

EPP 1.5-10
Rev. 6
May 3, 1986

BOULDER PETROCHEMICAL CORPORATION

GOLDEN REFINERY

Emergency Plan Procedure EPP 1.5-10

PREPARER ______________________

REVIEWER ______________________

____

OTHER REVIEWERS ______________________

____

PERSONNEL INJURIES

1.0 PURPOSE

To provide guidance for responding to personnel injuries during a plant and/or other medical emergency.

2.0 SCOPE

This procedure applies to the following Emergency Organization personnel:
- Director of Plant Emergency Operations
- Operations Shift Supervisor/Control Room Manager
- Security Director
- Public Information Officer
- Plant Medical Staff

3.0 REFERENCES

3.1 EPP 1.5-3, Notification and Communication
3.2 EPP 1.5-23, Director of Plant Emergency Operations
3.3 EPP 1.5-24, Security Director
3.4 EPP 1.5-27, Control Room Manager

4.0 DEFINITIONS

None.

Page 1 of 4

Figure 3-11. Sample Page 1 Showing Identification Information

issuing new procedure numbers should be strict. Moreover, some companies, when a procedure is canceled or superseded, retire that procedure's number indefinitely to avoid any possible confusion.

Here are some examples of procedure numbering systems:

Example 1

EOP-1 (the first in a series of emergency operating procedures)

Example 2

ADM 2.4-26 (administrative procedure, category 2, subcategory 4, 26th procedure in this subcategory)

Example 3

IP/2/A/7600/9 (instrument procedure, for Unit 2, category A, subcategory 7600, revision 9)

3.5.3 Page Identification and Numbering

Because most procedures are bound simply by a staple or by placement in a looseleaf binder, pages can be removed or lost. Certain pages may need to be deliberately removed to record data. Therefore, each page should contain full identification information:

- Page number
- Procedure number
- Revision number (if any)

Some companies also include the procedure title on every page. Others design a page format, such as is shown in Figure 3-12, that also includes the company name or logo and a full border. An advantage of this border is that the user can tell at a glance whether the text is complete or whether some words or lines may have been cut off in photocopying or printing.

A caution concerning page numbering: If a simple "1, 2, 3" system is used, indicate the final page of the procedure by the words "FINAL PAGE" or "LAST PAGE" under the page number

APC	ANCHOR PROCESSING PLANT		NUMBER
TITLE		REVISION	PAGE

Figure 3-12. Sample Page Format with Border

or "END OF PROCEDURE" after the last line of text. If the "1 of 25, 2 of 25" is used, no such indication is needed.

The procedure binding should be considered when positioning the page identification. For example, page identification in the upper left corner would be awkward or difficult to read if the procedure were stapled in that same corner.

Two common methods of page identification, in addition to that shown in Figure 3-12, are shown below:.

Example 1

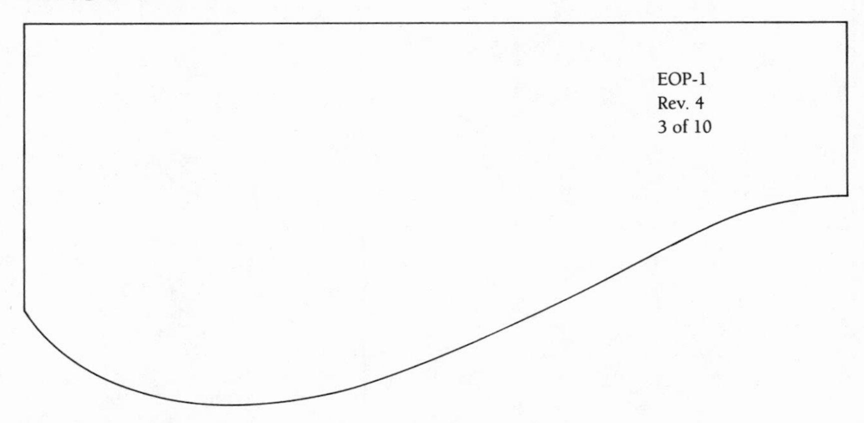

Example 2

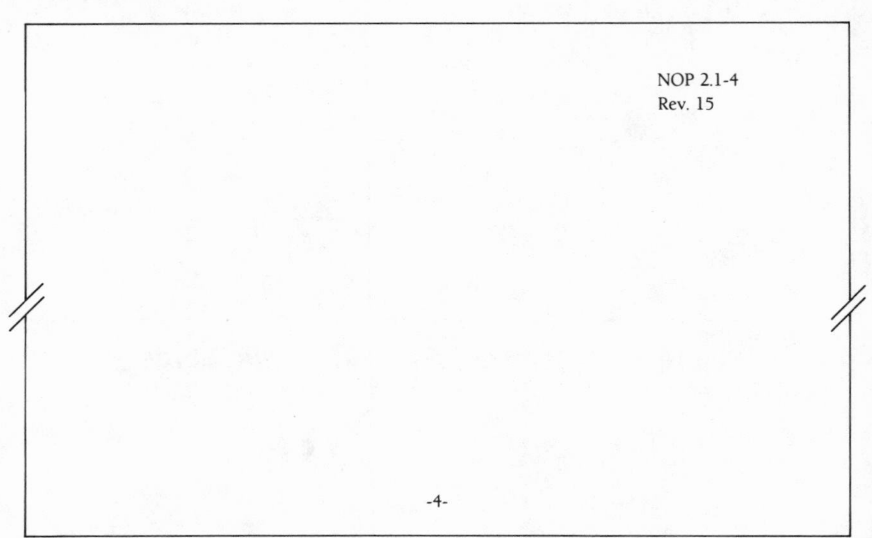

3.6 EFFECTIVE PARAGRAPHS

We have mentioned two basic types of procedures, administrative and technical. Both types of procedures describe a process. An administrative procedure on design control describes the process of controlling designs and design changes. An accounting department procedure on completing an expense report describes the task or process of completing the form. Technical procedures also describe a process or task.

Although the purpose of a procedure is by definition to describe a process or task, a few sections are descriptive in nature, such as a "System Description" section in a procedure on repairing that system. These sections may require a narrative style rather than the step-by-step style needed to give instructions. Any part of a procedure that describes a process should present its instructions in a step-by-step writing style with short sentences listed vertically. Any part of a procedure that is more descriptive requires a more narrative style, where one or more paragraphs are needed.

Therefore, two writing styles are used in procedures, the narrative style, which uses paragraphs, and the step-by-step style, which uses sentences listed vertically. The narrative style is discussed immediately below. The step-by-step style is discussed in the next section.

Having completed the planning stage, you should already know what sections of your procedure will require a narrative style. Now, in the drafting stage, you will need effective paragraphs to draft those sections of your procedure requiring a narrative.

3.6.1 Deductive Structure

In your planning product, by selecting major ideas and assigning minor ones to support them, you were developing a deductive structure for your procedure. "Deductive" simply means that we start with the more general idea or concept and then support it with related, more specific points or details. On the other hand, "inductive" means the opposite: You present your reader with several details that build to a general conclusion. Deductive and inductive structures apply to paragraphs also. These two types of paragraphs can be represented graphically as shown in Figure 3-13 below.

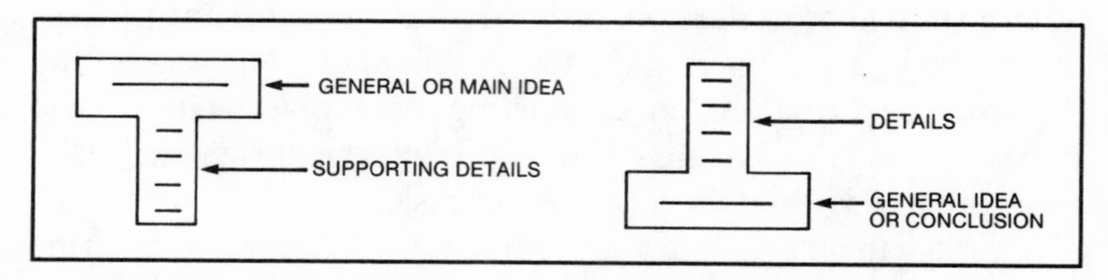

Figure 3-13. The Deductive versus Inductive Paragraph

In parts of procedures where narrative or description is needed, the deductive structure should be used. In fact, the deductive structure is appropriate for all types of technical writing—reports, letters, and memoranda.

The inductive structure is found in communication where the writer or speaker wants to build a case on details that lead unmistakably to a final conclusion. Public speakers, such as politicians, lawyers, and religious leaders, use the inductive structure. Mystery novels are inductive—the clues mount up until we reach the solution at the end of the book.

The inductive approach is not appropriate in procedures and other forms of technical writing, however, because it places too many demands on the reader. A paragraph organized inductively demands that the reader retain several details or specific points throughout the paragraph until the conclusion is finally reached. Then, if the reader is able to retain the details, he/she must then mentally review them to perceive the relationship between the details and the main idea.

Two characteristics of an effective deductive paragraph are unity and coherence.

3.6.2 Unity

Unity results when every sentence supports or explains the single focus established at the beginning of the paragraph. This focus is established by a topic sentence. The topic sentence should generally be the first in the paragraph. Occasionally, it may be the second sentence, if the first sentence is a transition from the previous paragraph. This topic sentence should state the main idea. Succeeding sentences should then support the main idea. This support may be developed in several different ways:

- Details, examples, and illustrations
- Comparison or contrast
- Cause and effect
- Chronological order
- Definition
- Classification or division

The most common method of paragraph development is to present details, examples, or illustrations. For example, a paragraph on a certain plant system may begin with the following topic sentence: "The condensate system contains four condensate pumps." The paragraph would then go on to name and describe the functions of the four pumps.

3.6.3 Coherence

Coherence results when the sentences within the paragraph flow easily from one to the next, leading the reader clearly and logically through the development of the main idea. Devices used by writers to help paragraph coherence are transition words. Used appropriately, these words improve the flow. However, coherence cannot be forced on a paragraph of unrelated ideas by use of transition words.

Table 3-1 shows transition words, their functions, and the kinds of paragraphs in which they are used.

A few words of caution on paragraph development:

- Avoid one-sentence paragraphs except as the closing paragraph of the section. Organize your material so that each paragraph has a main idea with at least one or two supporting details.

Table 3-1. Transition Words

Transition	Direction/Function	Paragraph Pattern
moreover, furthermore, in addition, also, besides, not only, another, next, likewise, then, first, second, until, when, before	Continuing the thought	• Details and examples • Time order
consequently, as a result, finally, therefore, in conclusion, in summary, hence, accordingly, due to, because, since	• Concluding the thought • Showing relationships	• Cause/effect • Comparison/contract • Time order
for example, specifically, for instance, in other words, that is	Illustrating the thought	• Details and examples • Cause/effect • Comparison/contrast
however, even though, although, but, yet, in spite of, because, whereas	Reversing the thought	• Cause/effect • Comparison/contrast

- Avoid paragraphs that are overly long. A good rule of thumb for maximum paragraph length is 9 to 11 lines (typed). It has been shown that the reader's attention and comprehension wane significantly beyond that point (Redish, 1985).

3.6.4 Examples of Deductive Paragraphs

The following is from a system description section in a turbine operating procedure:

> Turbine trips are caused by deviations of system variables in the steam and power conversion system. Significant malfunctions or conditions that cause turbine trips include:
>
> - Generator faults
> - Transformer faults

- Low bearing oil pressure
- Excessive wear on thrust bearings
- Turbine overspeed
- Turbine protection in case of generator motoring
- Low hydraulic oil trip
- Backup overspeed

The deductive structure of the above paragraph is further enhanced by the use of vertical format to present the details supporting the topic sentence.

The following is an excerpt from an administrative procedure on quality assurance audits:

> Before the internal audit schedule is approved and issued, the Safety Review Committee (SRC) reviews the schedule. This review is to verify that all corporate safety requirements are satisfactorily addressed and that any supplemental audits required by the SRC are scheduled. During the review, the SRC may make specific recommendations, such as the assignment of technical specialists or auditors for specific audits.

In the above paragraph, the SRC review named in the topic sentence is further described by the sentences that follow.

3.7 ACTION STEP CONSTRUCTION

The sentence structure used in a step affects the user's rate of comprehension. Short steps in a vertical format are more likely to be performed correctly than paragraph-style instructions. Moreover, after being interrupted, it is easier for a user to find his/her place in a vertical list than in the middle of a paragraph. Procedures written in short steps are also easier to edit, review, or revise.

Use the guidelines in the following subsections to construct steps that enhance user performance.

3.7.1 Use Simple Command Statements

Begin the sentence with an action verb followed by the object of the action:

THIS: Record reading.

NOT THIS: The reading must be recorded.

Omit the subject "you" in the sentence because it is implied in the imperative or command structure. Unnecessary articles (for example, a, an, or the) may be omitted, but should be included if clarity suffers. Other elements such as location or object modifiers are added as needed. For example:

	ACTION VERB	OBJECT	LOCATION
THIS:	Record	reading	on Data Sheet 1.

NOT THIS: Now you record the reading in the appropriate blank located on Data Sheet 1.

3.7.2 Keep Action Steps Simple

Three methods to keep action steps simple are discussed below.

Limit the Number of Action Verbs. Experts in human learning tell us that our short-term memory has definite limits, and that environmental conditions may affect it adversely. Therefore, action steps should be as simple as possible. The primary method of simplifying steps is to limit the number of actions. The more actions expressed in a step, the less likely the user will recall them accurately, thus introducing potential for error.

The readability factors of concept load and concept density are directly applicable here. You will recall from Chapter 2 that concept load refers to the number of ideas (actions) a user must read in a step, and concept density refers to how often complex steps appear in a procedure. High concept load and density increase the potential for error. Studies performed in nuclear power plant simulators have shown that when complex steps contain five actions, the fourth and fifth actions were not performed in 85 percent of the scenarios (Heuertz and Herrin, 1986).

Each procedure step should contain only one action. However, if two or three actions are related because they are performed virtually simultaneously or in close sequence, they should be included in the same step.

The number of actions in a step is indicated by the action verbs. The action verbs are in italics in the following examples:

- 6.8 *Verify* the "BOILER TRIP" lamp goes out.
- 5.16 *Depress* and *hold* the "TURB LATCH" pushbutton for about 2 seconds. *Verify* the "TURB LATCH" button stays lit and the "UNIT TRIP" lamp goes out.
- 3.8 *Direct* local operator to close the valve.

Step 6.8 contains one action instruction, "verify." Step 5.16 contains three action instructions, but they are all done in close sequence ("2 seconds," and then a moment to verify the status). Step 3.8 contains one action instruction, "direct," for the primary user of the procedure, in this case the control room operator. The phrase "to close" is not an action verb for the procedure's primary user; rather, it describes "what" the primary user must tell the local operator.

Now look at the following pair of examples:

Example 1:

6.3 *Wipe* rotating face body clean. *Install* U-cup in rotating face, *install* rotating face body over the shaft sleeve, and *engage* lugs on rotating face body in slots of U-cup follower. *Depress* rotating face body against spring holder assembly to check freedom of axial movement. *Verify* the movement is smooth and uniform.

Example 2:

6.3 *Wipe* rotating face body clean.

6.4 *Install* U-cup in rotating face.

6.5 *Install* rotating face body over the shaft sleeve.

6.6 *Engage* lugs on rotating face body in slots of U-cup follower.

6.7 *Depress* rotating face body against spring holder assembly and ***verify*** axial movement is smooth and uniform.

Example 1 is a single numbered step with six instructions. In addition, three of them, "install," "install," and "engage," are in one sentence. The procedure writer is risking user error here because of the heavy concept load. Example 2 breaks down the same step into simpler steps. Only Step 6.7 has more than one action verb because the "depress" and "verify" actions are performed in close sequence.

In the review stage (Chapter 4), we will look at a technique to analyze the complexity of the steps you have drafted. This technique, the Complexity Index, is an objective method that can be applied by you, the writer, or other reviewers.

Avoid Hidden Instructions. Sometimes an action instruction is hidden in the step because the writer chooses the wrong sentence structure to express the action. In this example, a verification instruction is hidden in the underlined portion.

> Turn on the synchroscope. The synchroscope should lock in the in-phase position.

The use of "should lock" does not clearly instruct the user and may cause the user to interpret. The user may ask: "and what do I do if it doesn't lock. . .?" The step should be reworded as follows:

> Turn on the synchroscope. Verify the synchroscope locks in the in-phase position.

Now the user knows exactly what to do. If the synchroscope does not lock in the correct position, the user follows the company's standard policy regarding steps that cannot be performed as written. Or, the writer may need to include a following step that tells the user what to do if the synchroscope does not lock in the correct position.

Keep Steps Free of Explanatory Information. A third problem that prevents steps from being as simple as possible is the inclusion of explanatory information within the action instruction. The numbered step should contain only the direct instructions. Look at this example:

> 8.4 *The inside of the pressure-reducing cell now forms the cavity for the secondary seal.* Install the split ring in the groove of the shaft sleeve.

The italicized sentence above is not an instruction, but a statement of information. Remember that a procedure is not a training manual. You may reconsider the training level of your least qualified user and decide that the italicized sentence is not necessary. However, if you do wish to provide this information as an aid or reminder to even the well-trained user, you should format the information in a note statement separate from the numbered step. Notes will be discussed later in this chapter.

We have discussed three ways that a writer can "clutter" a step: multiple action verbs, hidden actions, and explanatory information. As you draft your steps, be aware of these pitfalls that can detract from your procedure's usability.

3.7.3 Avoid the Passive Voice

In using the command structure described above, you will avoid a passive statement, which is a much weaker method of expressing the action. The first example below is preferable to the second:

THIS:	Set up the test box on the power panelboard.
NOT THIS:	The test box shall be set up on the power panelboard.

Studies of human learning and reading comprehension have shown that the reader pays the most attention and comprehends the best at the beginning of the sentence (Klare, 1975). This comprehension declines as the reader continues reading the sentence. Therefore, the most important word, the action verb, should come first. As you can see in the example of passive structure above, the word describing the action is the sixth word, not the first. The passive structure, "shall be set up" (a form of the verb "to be" plus a participle), prevents the action verb from being placed at the beginning of the step.

In addition to denoting precise actions, a procedure should also indicate the individual(s) responsible for performing each action. The use of passive voice can introduce a great deal of ambiguity into a procedure. When an action is written in the passive voice, the doer of the action is usually not identified in the step. The following example is from a quality assurance procedure that appears to be directed toward the inspector.

> Assure the proper method of tensioning the bolts has been performed. Bolts ***shall be brought*** to a snug-tight condition and either the turn-of-nut method or calibrated impact wrench method ***shall be used*** to tension the bolts. If the calibrated impact wrench is used, it ***shall be checked*** at least twice daily in a device capable of indicating actual bolt tension by tightening not less than three bolts for each size, grade, and condition being installed.

Does the inspector perform the italicized actions? Does a technician? The passive voice lends doubt as to who should perform the actions. Notice also the paragraph style. A step-by-step breakdown, in the active voice, would eliminate confusion.

3.7.4 Identify the Responsible Person

Your procedure is addressed to a primary user who is the "actor"; that is, this person is performing the actions. It is not necessary to state: "The technician shall. . .," "the operator shall. . .," or "the engineer shall. . ." for every step, as long as that primary user, your audience, is the actor.

However, if someone else is to perform the step, you must identify the actor. Look at the three examples below from a maintenance procedure:

INCORRECT:	Obtain a chemical sample.
STILL NOT ACCEPTABLE:	Chemistry Department shall take a chemical sample.

CORRECT: Have Chemistry Department take a chemical sample.

The first states that the maintenance technician, the primary user, is to take the sample, which is wrong. The second has the actor right, but the sentence structure is not the same as all the other steps; it is a declarative statement rather than an instruction telling the technician what to do. The third is the only correct instruction because it tells the technician to have another actor perform the action, which is what is actually intended.

3.7.5 Use Positive Statements

Phrase instructional steps so that they are positive rather than negative. Negative logic can be difficult to understand. The positive examples below can be more quickly and easily understood than the negative ones.

POSITIVE: If battery voltage is less than 125 VDC, record voltage value in Table 1.

NEGATIVE: If battery voltage is NOT less than 125 VDC, DO NOT record voltage value in Table 1.

POSITIVE: Run only one packing exhauster blower until enough seal steam flow is provided.

NEGATIVE: If seal steam flow is NOT sufficient, DO NOT run more than one packing exhauster blower.

3.7.6 State the Condition First

Conditional action steps involve a decision for the user. If a certain condition exists, the user performs an action. In this type of step, the action verb does *not* appear first. Here is an example:

> When documents containing Confidential information are no longer needed, shred the documents using the shredder in the controlled area.

Types of Conditional Steps. Two types of conditional steps are generally needed in a procedure: (1) a step where the action depends on an unexpected but possible condition, and (2) a step where an action depends on an expected condition. An "if" clause is used to express an unexpected condition; a "when" clause to express an expected condition. Look at the following examples:

> If water level cannot be maintained, go to Step 2.3.
>
> When pressure reaches 50 psig, perform Steps 6.5 through 6.8.

In the first example, the condition may never occur. In the second, the condition is expected to occur at some later point in the procedure.

Conditional Step Structure. The "if" or "when" clause (the condition) always precedes the action because the user needs this information to decide whether or when to perform the action. The "if" or "when" clause is followed by a comma. For example:

> If valve is motor operated, verify breaker is racked out and red tagged.
>
> When the form is completed, submit it to the Group Supervisor for approval.

Multiple Conditions. An action may be contingent on whether more than one condition exists. Especially where more than two conditions are involved, these steps must be written and formatted carefully to eliminate ambiguity or confusion.

If a combination of two conditions is required to perform an action, use the logic word AND to join the two conditions:

> If the stuffing box depth exceeds the five-ring height AND a split carbon sleeve is available, cut the split carbon sleeve to size and install it.

If either one of two conditions will initiate the action, use the logic word OR to join the two conditions:

> When significant changes are made in QA functional areas OR verification of a corrective action is needed, plant management shall request a Special Audit.

If three or more conditions are involved, a vertical format is preferable. In a vertical format, the comma following the conditional clause is not needed. Stringing three conditions together in a sentence is more difficult to comprehend than a list of conditions. The first example illustrates AND logic; the second, OR logic.

Example 1

WHEN ALL of the following conditions are indicated:

- Core exit thermocouples stable OR decreasing
- RCS hot leg temperature stable OR decreasing
- Steam generator pressure stable OR decreasing

THEN go to Step 6.3.

Example 2

IF any one of the following is in alarm condition:

- CC21 HEADER LO PRESS
- CC22 HEADER LO PRESS
- CC23 HEADER LO PRESS,

THEN go to Step 6.3.

The following example illustrates further emphasis on the logic words for the most critical situations.

IF any one of the following criteria is met:

- "CIS A & B TRIP" annunciators LIT

OR

- Pressurizer pressure less than 275 psig

OR

- "RCP VIB DANGER" annunciator LIT,

THEN stop the affected RCP.

Using AND and OR together in a conditional statement can be confusing. For example, the following instruction could be interpreted in more than one sense:

IF Condition A AND Condition B OR Condition C occurs, THEN go to Step 6.3.

Be sure to construct such instructions carefully so that the logic is clear. Here is one interpretation of the above example:

IF either one of the following occurs:

- Condition A plus Condition B
- Condition C,

THEN go to Step 6.3.

Use of Emphasis in Conditional Steps. When a conditional step requires special emphasis, the combinations IF. . ., THEN and WHEN. . ., THEN may be used, as in some of the examples above and the following:

> IF Closed Cooling Water Outlet Valve 2CCW31 CANNOT be closed from the control room, THEN send an operator to close the valve locally (Mechanical Penetration Area, 78 ft elev.)

In fact, nuclear power plants commonly apply this emphasis consistently in all their emergency procedures. With this exception, "if" and "when" need not be emphasized in every conditional statement, nor is it always necessary to begin the action portion with "then."

The logic words AND and OR are generally emphasized only where needed, according to the criticality of the step. A common method of emphasis is full capitals with underline, as shown in the above examples. (Methods of emphasis and their use are discussed in detail later in this chapter.) When "and" and "or" are used as simple conjunctions, they need not be emphasized, as in this example of a cautionary statement:

> Painting and staining may cause damage to the surfaces.

Negative Logic. Negative words such as NOT and IF NOT are often considered logic words also, in addition to IF, WHEN, AND, and OR. Again, depending on the need or criticality, these words may be emphasized, as in the following examples:

> If NONE of the valves will open. . .
>
> IF cooling water flow CANNOT be established. . .

The use of a conditional step (an "if" statement) does not necessarily require that the reverse condition be stated also (the "if not" situation). It is implicit that the procedure user continues to the next step when the condition expressed in the "if" statement does not exist. However, where the "if not" situation needs to be stated, this step should always follow the "if" statement rather than precede it. In other words, the positive precedes the negative, as shown in the following examples:

> If the purchase requisition is for safety-related equipment, go to Section 5.2.
>
> If the purchase requisition is NOT for safety-related equipment, go to Section 5.3.

3.7.7 List Multiple Objects Vertically

We earlier discussed building an action step by beginning with a verb, adding an object, and adding location or other information as needed. When an action verb has several objects, however, the chance of error increases as the number of objects increases. Reader comprehension and retention of information decline as a sentence lengthens. Therefore, attention to physical layout of the instruction, such as providing "space clues," will enhance performance accuracy.

A vertical format is a method of presenting three or more objects so that comprehension is enhanced. The following instruction can be improved using a vertical format:

> 6.3 Deenergize relays 16Z201A, 16Z205A, 16Z207A, and 16Z208A.

Written in a vertical format, the instruction would look like this:

> 6.3 Deenergize the following relays:
>
> - 16Z201A
> - 16Z205A
> - 16Z207A
> - 16Z208A.

If the list of objects is longer, consider two methods of presentation:

- Break the list into subgroups or columns of four or five.
- Format the list as a separate table to which the step refers the reader.

Another aid to the user is the addition of checkoff spaces. A small blank is provided next to each object so that users can check off as they complete the desired action on each object. For example:

6.3 Deenergize the following relays:

____ 16Z201A

____ 16Z205A

____ 16Z207A

____ 16Z208A.

In the first vertical list example above, "bullets" were used to designate the objects. Bullets may be used for lists when sequential order is not necessary. If the relays must be deenergized in that order, however, a numbering or lettering scheme ("1., 2., 3." or "a., b., c.") should be used. In addition, if sequential order is critical, the instruction should read "Deenergize the following relays in the order shown:"

The numbering scheme used to designate a list of objects should be distinct from the step hierarchy numbering scheme, especially where a multiple-digit method is used. The user expects to see discrete action instructions within the step numbering scheme, not merely lists of objects.

3.7.8 Use Parallel Structure

Parallel structure simply means that the same grammatical pattern has been used consistently at a given level—major headings, major tasks, steps, and so on. Parallel structure helps the user read and comprehend more quickly. When all steps are "in parallel," there are no surprises, and the user will not stumble over a step or have to stop and read a step again because it doesn't fit the pattern. Here are some examples:

Example 1

1. PURPOSE
2. SCOPE
3. DEFINITIONS

Example 2

10.1 Removal from Service

10.2 Repair

10.3 Return to Service

Example 3

10.2.1 Select the 5 amp scale on the text box.

10.2.2 Notify the control room of the possibility of a battery ground alarm.

10.2.3 Turn on the spare breaker.

Example 4 (not in parallel)

6.2.3 The engineering clerk shall forward the purchase requisition package to Quality

6.2.4 Quality Assurance shall review the purchase requisition package and return it to the engineering clerk.

6.2.5 The engineering clerk shall format the purchase requisition package in accordance with Attachment 2.

6.2.6 Records distribution is performed in accordance with Procedures OA-011 and OA-012.

In Example 1, these major section headings are parallel because they are all nouns. In Example 2, the major task names are all nouns and are therefore parallel. In Example 3, the steps are parallel because they are all commands beginning with verbs. A conditional step in such a sequence would still be in parallel because the verb is still in the form of a command.

Now, look at Example 4. Actions are directly stated in Steps 6.2.3, 6.2.4, and 6.2.5. Then the reader encounters a declarative statement in Step 6.2.6, with no clear direction as to who distributes the records. The solution is simple. We determined that the engineering clerk does in fact perform this step, so the step should be rephrased as follows:

6.2.6 The engineering clerk shall distribute records in accordance with Procedures OA-011 and OA-012.

Another common error is to mix major task headings with action steps at the same level. Once you establish an organization in which all items at a certain level are major tasks, you should avoid using this level for specific steps within that procedure. For example:

THIS: 11.1 Disassembly
(with substeps)

11.2 Cleaning

11.2.1 Clean metal parts with a clean wiping cloth and solvent PD320.

11.2.2 If solvent does not remove dirt, clean surface with compound DIC257 diluted with five parts water.

11.3 Paint Refinishing
(with substeps)

NOT THIS: 11.1 Disassembly
(with substeps)

11.2 Clean metal parts with a clean wiping cloth and solvent PDS20. If solvent does not remove dirt, clean surface with compound D1C257 diluted with five parts water.

11.3 Paint Refinishing
(with substeps)

Also, in a short procedure where the higher level is used for steps, you should avoid putting a heading in the step sequence.

3.7.9 Construct Steps Performed out of Sequence Properly

In most companies that use written procedures to accomplish tasks, the procedure user must perform every action step sequentially unless the procedure specifically states otherwise. Use the following guidelines to handle steps that are not sequential.

Nonsequential Steps. A step may require that an action be carried out at any time during a procedure. State clearly the conditions under which these steps apply. For example:

> If high pressure alarm sounds during this procedure, exit procedure and notify control room.

Equally Acceptable Steps. Equally acceptable steps are those for which alternative steps, methods, or equipment may be equally correct. If one method or piece of equipment is preferable, direct the reader to use alternatives only when necessary. However, if any alternative is equally acceptable, give the user the flexibility to use any of them. Here is an example:

Example 1

Energize the circuit by either of the following methods:

- Have Control Room Operator energize the circuit from the control panel.
- Energize the circuit locally by turning the test switches to "TEST."

Example 2

Start Auxiliary Feedwater Pump A. If Auxiliary Feedwater Pump A is not operable, start Auxiliary Feedwater Pump B.

Recurrent Steps. Recurrent steps require the user to repeatedly perform an action. State how often the step is to be performed and the conditions for no longer performing the step. For example:

> Repeat Steps 10.3 through 10.8 until the value is in tolerance.

Time-Dependent Steps. Time-dependent steps are required at a specific time interval, or some time after an action has taken place. Specify the time interval before the action. For example:

After 1 minute, reduce the pressure to 0 psig.

Concurrent Steps. Concurrent steps must be performed at the same time. Explicitly indicate which actions are concurrent within a step by using words such as "at the same time," "simultaneously," or "while." For example:

While applying 5 VDC, adjust the range potentiometer until the meter reads 100%.

If separate steps are concurrent, preface them with a note so that users will easily refer to both steps.

The maximum number of concurrent steps should not be beyond the capability of the expected number of users to perform them.

3.7.10 Use Informational Statements Appropriately

The procedural instructions are sometimes not adequate to fully guide the user in completing the task. Informational statements may be needed in addition to the step statements. Remember, however, that a procedure is not a training manual. The instructional section should contain a list of steps in the command format, with little explanatory material. Initial sections of your procedure—Purpose, Scope, System Description, etc.—are better suited to *brief* information on the procedure, such as its rationale or basis.

The level of detail also determines the amount of explanatory information needed. In the planning stage, you have analyzed the expected user(s). A user with minimum training and experience may better perform a procedure that gives explanatory notes, while a more experienced user may skip over such information.

Another factor affecting use of informational statements is the age of the facility or systems. A new manufacturing or power plant or a plant with new systems recently installed may need more detailed procedures with more informational statements. As a plant or system ages, subsequent procedure revisions may delete such information as it becomes common knowledge.

Informational statements should be formatted differently from the steps so that they are easily distinguished from the step sequence. These statements generally fall into two categories: cautions, which give safety-related information, and notes, which give helpful, but not safety-related information. These two types of statements are discussed separately below.

Cautions. A cautionary statement is most often called a caution, and is generally defined as information the user needs to prevent possible equipment damage or personnel injury. Some facilities have two levels of cautionary statements, called warnings and cautions, where warnings are reserved for extremely critical situations. Still others define a warning statement as relating to personnel safety, and a caution statement as relating to equipment safety.

- **Caution Content**. A caution should never contain a required action step; that is, the task instructions should be within the numbered step hierarchy. Users expect to see task steps in the numbered sequence. They do not expect to see them in cautions. In fact, a user thoroughly familiar with the task may skip over cautions, feeling that he or she is aware of any safety issues related to the task. If an action step is critical to the sequence, a caution is not the place for it. It should still be a numbered step, but emphasized or highlighted, such as with underlining or bold type. (Methods of emphasis should be consistently and sparingly used so that their effect is not minimized.)

  Thus, the sentence structure of a caution should not be a direct command or instruction such as "Ensure that retaining ring is seated on pinion shaft." This instruction should be a numbered step. Most cautions should be worded as a declarative sentence, that is, a statement of fact, such as:

High voltage gloves are required to make connections to the bus in Step 10.9.3.

A negative action statement is often used in caution statements also, such as:

DO NOT allow drycleaning solvent to contact skin.

A third type of caution statement used is the conditional statement. The majority of conditional statements should be numbered steps, however. A conditional statement is actually a decision point for the user. He/she must decide whether the condition exists before performing the action. If this decision/action is part of the required task sequence, it should be part of the step sequence, not a caution. However, if a conditional statement involves a safety issue (for personnel or equipment) affecting performing of the next step, it is better formatted as a caution. Here is an example:

If the stop valves begin to open during the next step, immediately trip the turbine.

A caution phrased as a conditional statement is also useful when the condition may occur at any time during the following step sequence and the user must retain the information while performing the following steps. The additional emphasis of the caution indicates that the user must remember the information. Some facilities use a distinct format for a caution that must be remembered during a series of steps or the remainder of the procedure. Here is an example from a flowchart procedure of a caution that must be remembered:

If Pressurizer level is lost during the following steps, DO NOT stop SG depressurization.

- **Caution Placement**. Regardless of how a caution statement is specifically defined, it should always be placed before the step to which it refers. If a caution appears after a step, the user may perform the step before reading the caution and thus may cause harm to personnel or equipment. For an electrical procedure step requiring the use of high voltage gloves, a caution stating that such gloves are needed would do little good following the step.
- **Caution Format**. As stated above, a caution should have a format distinct from the action steps. It should also appear more prominent than a note statement, described below. For example, a caution may be boxed, highlighted by rows of asterisks above and below it, or highlighted by bold type. The simplest method is to center the caution statement between margins and center the word CAUTION (or WARNING) above the statement. Here are some examples of cautions in single-column, multicolumn, and flowchart procedures.

Caution Examples: Single-Column Procedure

WARNING Compressed air used for cleaning should not exceed 15 psi, and then only with approved personnel protection equipment.

****

CAUTION

If retaining ring is not properly seated on pinion shaft,
damage to gearbox could result during operation.

****

WARNING

Relays 2B201 and 2B202 are energized as a result of Step 6.3.

Caution Example: Double-Column Procedure

ACTIONS	CONTINGENCY ACTIONS
CAUTION: A faulted or ruptured steam generator (SG) should remain isolated throughout further recovery actions.	
3.5 Check whether any SG is faulted.	3.5 IF any SG is faulted, THEN go to Step 3.51. IF all SGs are intact, THEN go to Step 3.52.

Caution Examples: Flowchart Procedures

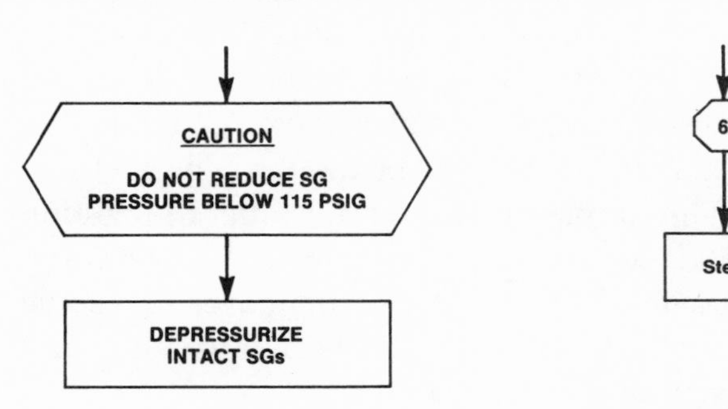

6. (Test of caution is shown in a list at bottom or on side of flowchart.)

Notes. A note statement is information that will help the user perform the step correctly or more efficiently. A note should never contain safety-related information.

- **Note Content**. As with the caution, a note should never contain a required action step. Users should be able to perform the procedure completely and correctly without reading any notes. However, the information in a note may improve performance accuracy, efficiency, or speed. A note is also a good device for adding brief explanations for action steps or brief descriptions of the results of action steps in a procedure that is performed by less experienced personnel.

  Two problems generally occur: (1) a note is hidden in a step and (2) a note is actually a hidden step. You will recall an example used earlier that illustrates the first problem:

4.4 The inside of the pressure-reducing cell now forms the cavity for the secondary seal. Install the split ring in the groove of the shaft sleeve, and insert the key into the key slot on the shaft sleeve.

The first sentence of Step 4.4 is actually a note. The key is the sentence structure. It is a declarative sentence, a statement of fact, not a command or instruction. This sentence should be formatted as a note.

Here is an example of the second problem:

Set 100% switch S-17 to "ON." The 100% lamp should illuminate on the PI panel in the control room.

In this step, the second sentence reads like a note, but is actually a step telling the user to verify that the lamp illuminates. This sentence should be rephrased, "Verify the 100% lamp illuminates on the PI panel in the control room."

In a procedure describing a series of discrete steps, use notes properly to ensure the user performs the procedure accurately.

- **Note Placement**. We said earlier that a caution always comes before the step to which it relates. Notes, however, may come before or after a step, depending on when the user needs the information in the step sequence. Generally, a note related to performing the step should be placed before it, but a note concerning the step results should be placed after the step. For example:

3.4 Request Technical Support Center to take additional action to prolong battery life.

NOTE: The Technical Support Center will estimate the time needed to restore power and the availability of portable power supplies, and will evaluate shedding nonessential DC loads.

In this example, a note concerning the Technical Support Center will make little sense to the user until he/she reads Step 3.4. Therefore, this note is best placed after the step.

- **Note Format**. A note should have a format that is different from the action steps, but not as prominent as a caution. A note does not need to be boxed or highlighted with bold type like a caution. A common note format is to precede the statement with "NOTE:" at the text margin. Here are some examples of notes in single-column, multicolumn, and flowchart procedures:

Note Example: Single-Column Procedure:

NOTE: Verification includes both the position indicator lights and position monitor lights.

Note Example: Double-Column Procedure:

ACTIONS	CONTINGENCY ACTIONS
3. Close all four isolation valves.	3. Send operator to close valves manually. NOTE: Table 4 lists valve locations.

Note Example: Flowchart Procedure:

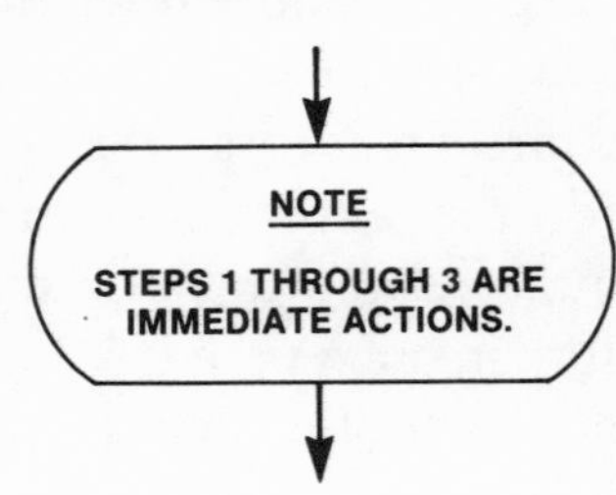

3.7.11 Use Appropriate Format and Wording for Referencing and Branching

You decided whether and where to use referencing and branching in the planning stage. You will recall that the term "referencing" means routing the user to other steps or sections within the same procedure or to another procedure, and after performing the referenced instructions, the user returns to the point from which he/she was referenced. However, the term "branching" means routing the user to another procedure or series of steps in the same procedure, and the user does not return to the initial procedure or step.

In the drafting stage, you should use specific verbs and a consistent format in phrasing the instruction to reference or branch.

Referencing Format. When referencing, use consistent wording and provide complete identification of the step, section, or procedure to be referenced. Some typical methods of wording are:

- . . . using AP.081, "Plant Procedures."
- . . . in accordance with OP.003, "Turbine Operating Procedure."
- . . . per Technical Specifications.
- Refer to M16-002, "Auxiliary Feedwater Pump Preventive Maintenance."
- Refer to Figure 1 for component part location.
- Document on Attachment 1.
- See Step 5.1 for as found readings.

If you reference a procedure more than once, it is cumbersome and may be unnecessary to repeat the title when that procedure is referenced a second time. Consider the user here. If a procedure is first referenced on page 4 and then not again until page 74, a full reference (number and title) on page 74 would be appropriate. However, the procedure number alone may be sufficient within a few pages of the first mention of the procedure number and title. In either case, the complete reference should have been listed in the References section.

Branching Format. As with referencing, you should use consistent wording and complete identification of the step, section, or procedure the user is to branch to. Typical verbs used for branching are:

- Go to
- Proceed to
- Return to
- Repeat

"Return to" would be used only for branching backward in the same procedure or branching back to a procedure that was in use earlier in the task sequence.

Very often, a branching instruction is part of a conditional step. For example:

3.5 If values are within tolerance, go to Step 3.7.

3.6 If values are *NOT* within tolerance, repeat Steps 3.1 through 3.4.

If the condition is true in Step 3.5, the user branches forward to Step 3.7. The user never performs Step 3.6. If the condition is not true, the user branches backward to Step 3.1 and begins again. The user will continue to loop backward to Step 3.1 until the condition of Step 3.5 is true; that is, the values are within tolerance.

When instructing the user to branch to another procedure, give complete identification—procedure number, title, and section number (if any). Keep in mind that you may need to direct the user to read the precautions of the branched procedure before he/she performs the section branched to. Here is an example of an instruction to branch to another procedure:

Go to OP-603.1, "Auxiliary Feedwater Pump Operation."

3.8 WORD CHOICE

The guidelines on action step construction discussed above have a common goal—to produce short, concise steps that enhance user performance rather than hinder it. In this section, we will look at the words that make up these steps. Issues related to your choice of words are the action verb; other vocabulary; equipment nomenclature; abbreviations, acronyms, and symbols used in place of words; and acceptance criteria.

3.8.1 The Action Verb

The verb is the most important word in a sentence. In fact, without a verb, a sentence becomes a fragment. In a procedure, the verb is crucial because it describes what you are asking the user to do. Therefore, the choice of verb to describe the desired action deserves attention. You should select a verb that precisely describes the action and then use it consistently in that context. Since procedure writing is not creative writing, you should deliberately use the same verb to describe the same action. Here are some examples of decisions that may be made and inconsistencies that can occur with the choice of action verb:

- Many process plants use "open" and "close" for valves consistently, rather than introducing the verb "shut" as an alternative to "close."
- The verb "replace" can have different interpretations. It can mean:

  — Replace the existing part with a new one.
  — Reinstall the same part that was removed.

  Therefore, care should be taken to specify exactly what is meant:

  — Install a new part . . ., OR
  — Install the original part . . .
- Some plants use "close" for valves and "shut" for breakers. In addition, "trip" a breaker may be used instead of "open" a breaker. In any case, consistency is the rule of thumb. Choose a verb and stick to it.

- When a procedure is to be read aloud to other personnel, you should avoid verbs that sound similar but actually are opposite in meaning. An example is "increase" versus "decrease." An alternative is to use "reduce" for "decrease."
- Several different verbs can be used to describe turning a switch to a certain position: "turn," "position," or "adjust." One verb should be selected and used consistently.
- Another case where several different verbs may be used is where other personnel must be asked to perform an action. Some of the possibilities are:
  — Have Chemistry sample. . .
  — Direct Chemistry to sample. . .
  — Notify Chemistry to sample. . .
  — Request Chemistry to sample. . .

  Again, one verb should be used consistently.

Your company or your department should maintain a list of recommended verbs to be used in procedures. Generally, a list of recommended verbs is needed for technical procedures at a minimum. The simplest verb is usually preferred; for example, "send" should be used instead of "dispatch."

3.8.2 Other Vocabulary

The words you use in procedures should reflect the ability, experience, and training of the expected users. Here are some specific guidelines.

Use Short, Commonly Found Words. You should use the simplest words possible, except where standard industry terms or technical words are necessary to define or clarify the subject. Many words and phrases have entered business and technical writing that are unnecessarily complex. Writers mistakenly think they are writing better when they use these expressions because they seem to sound more impressive. Certain other expressions are downright pompous; still others are overworked at best. Look at these examples and their simpler, more common versions:

- Prior to = before
- In lieu of = instead of
- Due to the fact that = because
- In the event that = if
- At that point in time = then
- Subsequent to = after

Overworked expressions that also contribute to vagueness and obscurity are:

- etc. (and so on, and others)
- i.e. (that is)
- e.g. (for example)

The expression "etc." automatically introduces imprecision and vagueness into a procedure, a document that strives to be precise in its language. Moreover, it is often redundant. Look at the following sentence:

> The Acme organization shall have project management responsibilities such as developing construction schedules, determining milestone dates, etc.

In this sentence, "etc." is redundant with "such as" and is not even necessary.

The expressions "i.e." and "e.g." are often confused by writers and users. Even if you, the writer, are clear on the distinction, you cannot be sure your user understands. Besides being confusing, these expressions are also overworked in technical writing. Use the English equivalents: "for example" instead of "e.g." and "that is" instead of "i.e."

Avoid Synonyms. Procedure writing is not creative writing; it is not necessary to vary your vocabulary. You should avoid synonyms, that is, different words that have a similar meaning. Consistently use the same word or term to describe a given subject, action, or object. We already discussed consistent action verbs above, but all other words in the sentence also need to be consistently used. For example, if a "rupture" is described in one step, the word "break" should not be used in a following step to describe the same phenomenon.

Use All-Inclusive Words with Care. All-inclusive words include:

- All, always, every
- Never, no, none

These definitive words are sometimes used carelessly. The user should be able to comprehend your procedure literally, not interpret it, as was discussed in Chapter 1. If you use "all," you are saying there is no exception to your statement. If in fact there may be an exception, the user is forced to interpret your wording and decide what to do.

Another issue is flexibility. Using all-inclusive words limits the flexibility your user has to get the job done correctly. On the other hand, the precision needed in procedures is hindered by every statement or step containing such phrases as "generally" or "normally." A balance must be struck between flexibility and clear, definitive instructions.

Of course, in a case where no exceptions are permitted, an all-inclusive word such as "never" or "all" is appropriate. Or, in a clear-cut instruction such as "Start *all* the pumps available," "all" is the correct word to use because "all" expresses the precise meaning.

Use Neutral Language. Many organizations have a policy, official or unofficial, discouraging the use of the male pronoun and its derivatives. This policy generally covers two areas, job titles and written documents.

- **Job Titles**. Many foremen are now "supervisors"; repairmen are now "technicians" or "repairpersons." Waiters and waitresses may be "servers," and stewards and stewardesses are "flight attendants." In a procedure, the correct organizational title must be used, whether it contains a masculine term or not. It is not up to the procedure writer to create new job titles for the organization. On the other hand, part of your research at the planning stage should have been to determine the correct job titles for the procedure you are writing. Then you can be sure that your procedure uses the correct personnel-related terminology.

- **Written Documents**. Your organization may discourage or even prohibit using masculine terms in documents. If your procedure is directed to one primary user, your instructions will be in the imperative or command form, and you will not need to use "he," "him," or "his." If your procedure involves several people, you may need to be more conscious of the masculine terms if your organization's policy is to avoid them.

  The following are a few ways to attack this problem.

  — Make the person plural. Rather than saying "The technician shall contact his supervisor," make the sentence plural: "Technicians shall contact their supervisor."

  — Repeat the noun instead of using the male pronoun:

    Notify an instrument technician and have the technician (instead of "him") remain on standby until job completion.

    Repeating the noun may be too cumbersome in some sentences.

  — Use one of the following methods instead of the masculine terms:

    - he or she, him or her
    - he/she, him/her

  This method is probably the most awkward when used a great deal in a document. It should be used sparingly. You should also consistently use either "he or she" or "he/she" and not mix the terms in your document. In fact, the entire procedure system should use the same term.

- — Compounds using the word "man" have the following neutral equivalents:
  - Manpower = personnel
  - Man-hours = work-hours or simply hours

Use Proper American Usage. Many writers have the technical knowledge to write a procedure on a given task, but may use nontechnical words incorrectly. For example, the following are often used incorrectly:

- Affect/effect
- Principal/principle
- Ensure/insure
- Comprise/compose

Appendix A lists words commonly used in procedures with clarifying explanations and examples of their correct usage. In addition, the bibliography contains several references on American usage. Keep such a reference handy while you are writing.

Use "Shall," "Should," and Similar Words Appropriately. A procedure by definition describes the required or at least preferred method of performing a task. A procedure contains requirements or recommendations related to the task itself and the personnel performing it (or ensuring that it is performed). The procedure instructions must use precise words to indicate to the user whether an instruction is a requirement.

In the nuclear power industry, much research has been devoted to plant procedures to determine how they can be improved to prevent or at least not contribute to user performance errors. This research has resulted in virtually universal use of certain verbs to denote levels of requirements. In fact the American National Standards Institute and the American Nuclear Society have defined "shall," should," and "may" in ANSI/ANS-3.2-1982, "Administrative Controls for Quality Assurance for the Operational Phase of Nuclear Power Plants," as follows:

- Shall = a requirement
- Should = a recommendation
- May = an option

Most nuclear power plants follow this standard in the use of these verbs so that users clearly understand whether a step is a requirement or a recommendation. Your facility should define the terms used in procedures so that all users are clear on the intent of the instruction.

Look at the following steps:

> ***Install*** retaining ring on pinion shaft.
>
> Project Management ***shall prepare*** all revisions to this procedure.
>
> The technician ***must take*** the following equipment out of service.
>
> The audit team ***will conduct*** a brief pre-audit conference with the organization's management.
>
> The Supervisor ***reviews*** the work schedule daily to ensure items are completed on time.

All of the above statements could be read (or misread) as required steps. Consistency is vital. The command style of step, "Install. . .," is generally considered a requirement, as is a statement containing "shall." The difficulty occurs when a user encounters other verb forms such as "must take," "will conduct," or "reviews" and must decide whether they are requirements. In particular, "shall" and "will" are erroneously used interchangeably. "Must" is used less frequently. The present tense, "reviews," may be read as a requirement or as merely a statement of fact.

Your facility should determine the wording it will use to denote a requirement and train users on the meaning of this wording. If certain words may be used interchangeably to express a requirement, such as "shall," "will," and "must," your facility should state this fact in documents controlling procedures. If the present tense, such as "The Supervisor reviews. . ." indicates a requirement for the Supervisor rather than simply a description of the Supervisor's function, such use of the present tense should also be specified.

Now look at these steps:

> A temperature survey ***should be performed*** before working in a hot environment.
>
> Auditors ***may perform*** unannounced audits at any time.

The first step uses the word "should," which according to conventional use in the nuclear power industry, indicates a strong recommendation but not necessarily a requirement. Some plants indicate that in theory a "should" statement does not have to be performed, but in practice it is essentially a requirement.

The second step above uses "may perform." "May" indicates an optional step that is up to the user's discretion.

You should be careful not to weaken a required instruction with such phrases as "if required." Such phrases directly contradict the intent of "shall." Where such qualifying phrases are needed, using "should" makes more sense.

In summary, no matter what the type of procedure, no matter what type of industry you are writing for, you should determine your organization's interpretation of:

- Command sentence structure
- Shall, will, or must
- Present tense
- Should
- May

If the organization has a definite policy, consistently follow it. Within a given procedure, consistently use the same word to describe a requirement, even if your organization uses interchangeable words. In other words, if you begin describing a required step by stating, "The Design Engineer shall," and then switch to "The Engineering Clerk will," the user may be confused as to what is required, particularly because "will" also indicates future performance.

If your organization has not clarified the use of these words, it should do so, so that all procedure writers and users correctly understand their meaning as to the level of requirement.

3.8.3 Equipment Nomenclature

In a technical procedure dealing with plant equipment, you must identify that equipment correctly and completely so that the user can identify it. In addition, you should also specify the equipment's location in many cases.

In a nontechnical procedure, the "equipment" may be a certain document or form. You should still take care to specify the correct title of the document and the correct number and title of the form.

Two methods may be used to identify equipment. Each is appropriate in certain cases.

Verbatim or Nameplate Identification. This method of nomenclature is best used where the user may be confused between similar pieces of equipment. For example, control room panel labels sometimes differ by only one letter or a number, so the exact verbatim label is essential to the user. The commonly used term for the equipment controlled by the button or switch on the panel may not be specific enough for the user to select the correct button or switch. Verbatim nomenclature is presented in full capital letters as it is normally found on control panels or equipment nameplates. Here are some examples:

CNDST PMP (condensate pump)

BRG OIL HDR (bearing oil header)

A special case where verbatim nomenclature is also used is when stating alarm or annunciator legends in control room procedures. Such legends are presented in full capital letters, as they are on the alarm windows, and may also be enclosed in quotation marks. The quotation marks serve as a method of highlighting the alarm legend. Some examples are:

"TURB TRIP"

"CC21 HEADER LO PRESS"

Official Equipment Name. This method is the most commonly used in procedures. The difference between this method and the verbatim method is that abbreviations found on the nameplate or control panel are spelled out. For example, a CNDST PMP in verbatim nomenclature becomes a condensate pump when spelled fully. The official equipment name usually is the same name the user uses to describe the equipment, because the user should have been trained to know the names of the plant equipment. If technicians actually use informal or incomplete terminology to identify equipment, you must consider whether such informal terms would be appropriate in a written procedure. Chances are that the least qualified user, the newest employee, may not be familiar with informal terms. Although procedures must be easy for the user to comprehend, they must also be technically accurate. Therefore, informal or slang nomenclature is generally not precise enough for procedures. The official names of major plant systems are often initially capitalized. Some organizations also initially capitalize the names of major system components. However, generic terms such as wrench or screwdriver need not be capitalized. See the following examples:

Turbine Lube Oil System

Condensate System

gearbox

bearing

gasket

3.8.4 Equipment Location Information

Location information should be given for equipment that is:

- In out-of-the-way places
- Difficult to find
- Seldom used
- Not labeled or labeled inconspicuously

You should use a consistent method of stating equipment location. For example, if the building name, elevation, and room number must be stated for several different items, consistently state this information in the same order each time.

3.8.5 Acronyms and Initialisms

The complex terms used to describe plant systems and equipment and company departments, committees, and documents are often converted to acronyms and initialisms in verbal and written applications. Acronyms and initialisms are formed from the initial letters of each part of a compound term. An acronym is pronounced verbally as a word, such as NATO (North Atlantic Treaty Organization), while each letter of an initialism is pronounced individually, such as EPA (Environmental Protection Agency). In this discussion, the term acronym refers to both acronyms and initialisms.

Using acronyms in procedures is entirely appropriate. In more formal writing, it may be more appropriate to use the full nomenclature. Your main concern as a procedure writer is that the acronym is commonly used in your organization and that the item is more likely to be referred to in practice by the acronym than its full name. Even if the acronym's meaning is common knowledge, you should still define it the first time it is mentioned in a procedure. For example:

motor operated valve (MOV)

Temporary Change Notice (TCN)

The full name of the acronym is initially capitalized only when it is a proper name. It does not need to be initially capitalized merely because the acronym letters themselves are capitals.

Some other guidelines in using acronyms are:

1. Define an acronym that may not be widely known by your audience in a Definitions section. Even though it is spelled out once, the user may not remember its meaning all the way through the procedure. If the Definitions section contains the acronym, the user can easily locate its meaning.

2. In a very long procedure, more than 25 pages for example, consider redefining acronyms in each major section to help the user remember their meaning. This method

would be needed for acronyms that are not commonly known by all of your users.

3. Consistently spell acronyms the same way. In past years, acronyms were often spelled with periods, for example PR (purchase requisition) would have been P.R. As our language evolves, periods are disappearing from acronyms. An older procedure or document may use P.R., while a recent procedure may use PR. Or, the same procedure may inconsistently use both. You should consistently use the same acronym for the same equipment or item name.

   Another inconsistency occurs when combinations of acronyms and words are used interchangeably with full acronyms, for example:
   - For auxiliary feedwater pump: AFW pump or AFWP
   - For reactor coolant pump: RC pump or RCP

   Again, be consistent in your nomenclature. Imprecise or inconsistent wording may momentarily confuse your user.

4. Make acronyms plural by adding a lower case "s." Do not use an apostrophe with an s (upper or lower case) to make an acronym plural. Reserve the apostrophe to indicate possession. Here are some examples:
   - PRs, not PR's for plural
   - AFWPs, but "The AFWP's controls are located on Panel C1813."

3.8.6 Abbreviations

An abbreviation is a shortened version of a word, as distinguished from an acronym, which consists of the initial letters of a compound term. The most common abbreviations used in procedures are engineering units and other units of measure. Other abbreviations are those found on equipment nameplates or control panels. These abbreviations are used in procedures where verbatim nomenclature is needed. Examples are:

- TEMP for temperature
- PRESS for pressure
- ISOL for isolation
- VLV for valve

However, these abbreviations are not used in the text of procedures unless they are representing verbatim nomenclature.

Engineering units and other units of measure should be used according to the following guidelines:

1. Standard abbreviations for units should be used. Consistent use of a dictionary of technical terms will ensure that correct abbreviations are used.
2. Abbreviations for units need not be spelled out at their first use in a technical procedure, because the basic technical training of the procedure users should cover the use of these abbreviations. However, if there is any doubt that the user understands the abbreviation, it should be defined in a definitions section or spelled out when first used.
3. Abbreviations for units need not be made plural. For example, the abbreviation "lb" denotes either pound or pounds, so it is not necessary to state "lbs" for pounds.
4. Like acronyms, most abbreviations for units do not contain periods. An exception is the abbreviation "in." for inch, to avoid confusion with the word "in." Here are some examples:
   — ft (feet)
   — psi (pounds per square inch)
   — gpm (gallons per minute)
   — min (minutes)
   — ft-lb (foot-pounds)
5. If a standard abbreviation may be confusing to the user, it is better to use the word or adopt another method of abbreviating that unit within your organization. An

example is the unit of time, "second." Some technical dictionaries give the abbreviation "s" for "second." Many procedure users have found this abbreviation to be confusing or at least not immediately recognizable as "seconds." Therefore, the abbreviation "sec" is often used. Another example is "ampere." Many organizations use the abbreviation "amp" instead of "A" for ampere because it is less confusing.

3.8.7 Symbols

Mathematical symbols are often used in technical procedures to achieve brevity or to save space in tables. Two cautions apply:

- The meaning must be immediately understandable to the least qualified user.
- The symbol must remain clearly recognizable through typing and generations of photocopying.

As an example of the first caution, consider the following symbols:

$<$ (less than)

$>$ (greater than)

$\leq$ (less than or equal to)

$\geq$ (greater than or equal to)

Even though the user may have been trained to understand and distinguish among these symbols, under certain conditions such as physical stress or a time limit on the procedure, the user may misinterpret them. Some organizations use the words rather than the symbols in the procedure text, but then permit the use of these symbols in supporting tables or data sheets. Thus, if the user is momentarily confused when referring to the table, the user can clarify the item by rereading the procedure step.

Examples of the second caution are these symbols:

′ (foot or feet)

″ (inch or inches)

In addition to the possibility of misinterpretation by the user, these symbols do not stand up well to multiple generations of photocopying. Even though the original typed copy may be clear, the chances are good that these symbols will become blurred.

3.8.8 Acceptance Criteria

Acceptance criteria tell the user what to look for to determine whether the step has been accomplished correctly. The two types of acceptance criteria are qualitative and quantitative. These criteria may be stated within the step, or they may be set out separately in a table or data sheet, or even in a separate section titled "Acceptance Criteria."

All acceptance criteria must be specific. Use the following guidelines:

1. For qualitative acceptance criteria, explicitly indicate what should occur (or not occur) to ensure acceptability. Avoid vague words like "normal" and "satisfactory."
2. Specify quantitative values in units compatible with the units on the equipment.
3. Use values that are readable on instruments and meters. The most precision with which the user can read values is generally one-half the distance between markings.
4. When the user must calculate a value, provide numerical or graphical acceptance criteria against which the value is to be compared.

Here are some examples of methods of presenting acceptance criteria in a procedure:

- Qualitative acceptance criteria within a procedure step:

  Position shims under the sill plate until the sill plate is level.

  Close Feedwater Isolation Valve FWI 2316.

  In the first sentence, the criterion is explicitly stated (the sill plate must be level). In the second sentence, the criterion is implied (the valve must close). In this instance, the procedure goes on with contingency instructions if the valve does not close.

- Quantitative acceptance criteria stated within the step:

  Maintain maximum auxiliary feedwater flow until at least one steam generator level is greater than 5%.

  Throttle Steam Seal Bypass Valve MS10 to obtain a normal pressure of 1 to 4 psig.

  Both of the above examples give quantitative values as acceptance criteria.

- Acceptance criteria presented in a table or data sheet:

Example 1: In a Table

6.1.3 Pull back on the spring scale. Note the point where the clutch slips and record the value in the As Found blank of the table below.

NOTE: The clutch should normally slip between 50 and 60 lb, but in no case should the clutch setting exceed 170 lb.

6.1.4 If adjustment is needed, adjust the clutch setting and record the As Left value below.

Clutch Setting		
As Found	As Left	Acceptance Criteria
______	______	170 lb

Example 2: On a Data Sheet (shown as "Required Output")

Input (% of Span)	Required Output (psi)	As Found (psi)	As Left (psi)
0	3.0 (2.97 - 3.03)		
25	9.0 (8.73 - 9.27)		

In these examples, the acceptance criteria are adjacent to the blank where the user fills in the value obtained, so the user can immediately determine whether the value is acceptable. This format is also convenient for a reviewer who must determine whether the task was performed correctly, because the actual value and the acceptance criteria can be easily compared.

- Acceptance criteria shown in a separate section:

  11.0 ACCEPTANCE CRITERIA
  Reactor Engineering has evaluated the flux map and determined that no anomalies exist in the core power distribution that would result in adverse power peaks during full power operation.

3.8.9 Tolerances

A special type of acceptance criterion used often in procedures is the tolerance. Instead of giving one specific value as the acceptance criterion, the procedure gives a range of values considered normal or acceptable for completion of the step. This range is the tolerance range.

Two types of tolerances are the acceptance range and the nominal value with tolerance range. All tolerances should be presented in immediately understood units that match those on the plant equipment or instrumentation from which the user must read the value. The user should not have to interpret or convert the acceptance criteria, but apply them directly to the task.

Acceptable Range. If there is no specific desired value, provide the tolerance as a range. For example:

> Verify pump temperature is within operating band of 450° to 485°F.
>
> Maintain steam generator narrow range level between 15% and 33%.

Nominal Value. For desired or nominal values, specify the value followed by a range of acceptable tolerance within parentheses. For example:

THIS:	Adjust current to 5 ma (4.25 to 5.75 ma).
NOT THIS:	Adjust current to 5 ± 0.75 ma.
NOR THIS:	Adjust current to 5 ma ± 15%.

The use of ± with a nominal value is asking the user to perform addition and subtraction before the user can determine whether the acceptance criterion has been met. Again, the user must interpret what the procedure writer means in order to complete the task. The above example with 15% requires even more interpretation because the user must perform multiplication to determine the range. It is very likely that written calculation would be required in this case.

3.9 MECHANICS OF STYLE

As we discussed at the beginning of this chapter, we are approaching the drafting stage deductively. First we examined the different methods of format and document design that can be used in procedures. Then we reviewed effective paragraphing. We next discussed action step construction, including how to build a typical action step using a verb, an object, and location or other supporting information. In the previous section we looked at word level concerns such as action verbs and specific acceptance criteria. Now we are ready for the finest level of detail, mechanics of style.

The term "mechanics of style" generally refers to spelling, capitalization, and punctuation. Here we will discuss these issues as they relate to procedures, and we will also deal with methods of emphasis and the use of numerals, including the presentation of formulas and calculations in procedures.

3.9.1 Spelling

Spelling should be based on a current American dictionary. Preferably, all writers in your organization should use the same dictionary, because the spelling and the division of syllables of certain words do vary among dictionaries.

Not all spelling questions can be solved by using dictionaries. Many compound terms are not listed in dictionaries, and the question is usually whether to write the term as two words, spell it as one word, or hyphenate it. Examples are the terms "off site" and "on site." Look at the following sentences:

> Procedures are published on site.
>
> Procedures are published by an on-site reproduction department.
>
> Procedures are reviewed onsite and then published by an offsite copy center.

In the first sentence, "on site" is an adverbial phrase telling where the procedures are published; therefore, it is two words. In the second sentence, "on-site" is an adjective describing the reproduction department, so the two words are linked by a hyphen. This type of term is called a unit modifier because two or more words are linked by hyphens to form a unit that modifies a noun.

In the third and fourth sentences, "onsite" and "offsite" are spelled as one word regardless of how they are used in the sentences. In this case, the organization has made a style decision to spell both these terms as one word at all times.

In such "gray" areas where the dictionary does not give us a definitive answer, inconsistencies will abound if we do not standardize spelling within an organization. Even where the dictionary does offer a spelling, if this spelling appears to confuse the user, procedure writers may decide to alter that spelling within the procedure system. Common examples are words where the prefix and the root word cause two vowels to come together and the resultant word may be misread or at least cause some hesitation. Two such words are "deenergize" and "reenergize." Although current dictionaries show these spellings to be correct, many procedures use the hyphenated spelling for clarity: "de-energize" and "re-energize."

The goal is consistency. Where two spellings of a term are in common use, decide on one method of spelling and use it exclusively.

3.9.2 Capitalization

Standard rules of capitalization should be followed in procedures. However, many capitalization rules cannot be called standard. Again, the goal is consistency. Your organization should establish basic guidelines to achieve consistency within the procedure system.

Many procedure writers have a tendency to capitalize (that is, initially capitalize) too many terms in procedures. Or, they capitalize a major component in one step, but do not in a later step. Capitalization is like a method of emphasis: If used too often, it does not accomplish its purpose and may even hamper reading speed and comprehension. Inconsistent capitalization may also confuse the user.

Here are some basic guidelines for capitalization in procedures. (Using capitalization as a method of emphasis will be discussed in the next section.)

1. Always initially capitalize (that is, capitalize the first letter of) the important words in the following:
   - Proper nouns, such as the organization's name:
     Forest Grove Electric Station
     Horizon Chemical Company

- Official personnel or staff titles:
  Senior Shift Supervisor
  Project Engineer
  but: mechanic or clerk
- Document titles (use quotation marks for the titles)
  Plant Operations Directive 25, "Procedure Control and Revision"
  Columbia Manufacturing Company, "Butterfly Valve Installation and Repair"

In the above situations, the important words in the title or name are always initially capitalized. To avoid inconsistency in capitalization of the remaining words, use the following guidelines:

- Capitalize the first and last word of the title.
- Capitalize all nouns and verbs.
- Do not capitalize articles (a, an, the), conjunctions (and, or, etc.), or prepositions (with, on, between, etc.).

The length of the word does not determine whether it should be capitalized, but its function in the sentence.

2. Always initially capitalize:
   - The first word in a sentence
   - The first word in procedure steps and substeps
   - The first words of items in a list
   - Words such as Step, Section, Figure, or Table when followed by a designating numeral:

     Step 6.5
     Section 4.0
     Figure 1
     Table 4
3. Initially capitalize:
   - Each word in a major system name:
     Emergency Cooling Water System

- Each word in official equipment or component nomenclature:
  Auxiliary Feedwater Pump
- Each word in terms expressing modes or conditions of plant operation:
  Startup, Standby, Shutdown
- Important words in procedure subsection headings:
  "Removal from Service"

4. Write the following in full capital letters:
   - Equipment nomenclature copied exactly from the nameplate or control room panel
   - Alarm or annunciator legends copied exactly from the alarm window (quotation marks are often used also)
   - Major procedure section names, such as PURPOSE or REFERENCES (often underlined also)
   - Informational statement designators, such as CAUTION or NOTE (often underlined also)

3.9.3 Methods of Emphasis

Procedure writers need to emphasize certain words and phrases to ensure the user performs a step correctly. Methods of emphasis to highlight Cautions and Notes have already been discussed. Within procedure steps, emphasis techniques should be used consistently and sparingly so that their effect is not minimized. Use the following guidelines (bold type may be used instead of underline):

1. Use full capitals and an underline for important logic words: AND; OR; IF. . ., THEN; WHEN. . ., THEN
2. Use full capitals and an underline for negative words: NOT, NEITHER, NOR, NONE
3. Within a procedure step, use full capitals or full capitals with underline to highlight important words:

Turn switch to BYPASS position.
Start No. 3 AFWP ONLY.

4. Within a flowchart-style procedure typed in full capital letters, use underlining, quotation marks, and bold type for emphasis.
5. Avoid mixing emphasis techniques. For example, "and" may be emphasized in any of the following ways:

   AND
   AND
   and
   AND
   and

   One method should be chosen and used consistently.
6. Use caution when using full capitals for emphasis in the same sentence with acronyms. The emphasized word is difficult to distinguish from the acronym. For example:

   THIS: Start No. 3 AFWP ONLY.
   NOT THIS: Start No. 3 AFWP ONLY.

3.9.4 Punctuation

You should use standard American English rules for punctuation. Remember, your goal is clarity and readability. Incorrectly used punctuation can change your intended meaning.

Punctuation marks are listed alphabetically below with examples of correct usage.

Apostrophe

- Use an apostrophe to indicate possession:
  mechanic's tool kit
- An apostrophe is used to indicate a contraction (for example, can't, don't, it's). Avoid contractions in procedures to eliminate confusion, such as having to distinguish between it's and its.

- Avoid the use of apostrophes to indicate plurals, especially with acronyms. For example, use PRs (purchase requisitions) as the plural of PR.

Brackets

- Use brackets only as required in mathematical equations and formulas.
- Avoid using brackets in the procedure text. Many word processing systems cannot print brackets.

Colon

Use a colon to indicate a series or list:

Evaluate need for the following systems:

- Cooling Water
- Primary Makeup
- Main Generator Hydrogen Control
- Control Air

Comma

- Use a comma to set off an introductory clause or phrase:
  Upon receipt of a draft from Engineering, review for proper format.
- Use a comma after the "if" or "when" clause in a conditional statement:
  If the procedure is safety related, forward to the Plant Safety Review Committee.
- Use a comma to separate items in a series. Be sure to include the comma before the conjunction. Although current American business writing style is to delete the serial comma, use it in procedures to ensure clarity and avoid user misinterpretation:
  Sign, date, and return the review request to Engineering.
- Use a comma to separate elements for clarity or emphasis:
  . . . go to SOP 16.002, "Turbine Operating Procedure," Section 5.2.

- Use a comma to separate five or more digits: 20,000 ppb

Exclamation Point

Avoid the exclamation point in procedure writing. Use other methods of emphasis.

Hyphen (-)

- Use a dictionary to determine those words that must be hyphenated. If the term is not given in your dictionary, determine the most common spelling used at your facility and use it consistently.
- Use hyphens to indicate syllable breaks where a word must be carried over from one line to another. Wherever possible, avoid breaking words, especially in the procedure's instructional section.

THIS:	Pipette the sample into a 250 ml flask. Dilute with distilled water to 100 ml, and add 2 to 3 drops of methyl red.
NOT THIS:	Pipette the sample into a 250 ml flask. Dilute with distilled water to 100 ml, and add 2 to 3 drops of methyl red.

- Do not hyphenate words with the following prefixes unless misleading or awkward letter combinations result:

- pre	- micro
- post	- mini
- re	- multi
- sub	- non
- super	

Parentheses

- Use parentheses to set off explanatory or supplementary information: sodium chloride (NaCl).
- Never enclose an action instruction in parentheses because they indicate that the enclosed words are of lesser importance.

- Specify an acceptable range or tolerance in parentheses following a nominal or desired value: 225 psig (220-230 psig)

Period

- Use a period at the end of a complete sentence.
- DO NOT use periods in:
  — Acronyms: PR, not P.R.
  — Abbreviated units of measure: lb, not lb. (Exception: use in. for inch)
  — Lists where the items are not complete sentences

Question Mark

Use a question mark with the yes/no question at decision points (diamond symbol) in flowcharts.

Quotation Marks

- Use quotation marks to set off alarm and annunciator legends: "CC21 HEADER LO PRESS."
- Use quotation marks to set off titles of documents referred to in procedure steps:
  Conduct calibration in accordance with Bennington Technical Instruction, "Calibration of Bennington Cast Steel Valves."
- Regardless of the logic of the sentence, place a period or comma inside a closing quote. Place other punctuation marks inside or outside the closing quote, depending on the logic of the sentence. For example:

THIS:	Refer to Procedure SOP.2.001, "Boiler Operation."
NOT THIS:	If the following alarm sounds: "DIESEL GEN SUMP A HI LVL", go to Step 11.2.2.

Semicolon

Generally, avoid semicolons in procedures because they encourage long sentences.

Slants

Use slants with units of measure to indicate "per": lb/hr.

3.9.5 Use of Numerals

The use of numerals versus words can be difficult to handle for maximum clarity and consistency. Apply the following guidelines, which are generally used in technical writing:

1. For units of measure, distance, and time, use the numeral rather than the word:

225 psig	47 ft
500 gpm	5%
5 minutes	3 miles

2. In all other cases, spell out the word if nine and under; use the numeral for 10 and above:
   three operators
   10 procedures
3. Where combinations of numbers are needed, use words and numerals for clarity: eleven 3-kg packages.
4. DO NOT repeat a spelled-out number in parentheses:
   THIS: three operators
   NOT THIS: three (3) operators
5. For numbers less than one, precede the decimal point by a zero: 0.5.
6. Ensure that the number of significant digits specified in the procedure is equal to the number of significant digits the user can read from the display on the instrument. For example, if the procedure specifies 7.006, the instrument must read out in one-thousandths.
7. Use the units of measurement that actually appear on the instrument.
8. Avoid operations that require conversions between equivalent sets of units. Where conversions are necessary, provide graphs, charts, or tables where the desired value can be obtained without calculation.
9. Never begin a sentence with a numeral.

10. If a sentence contains two or more numbers (not units of measure) of which at least one number is 10 or greater, use numerals for all of them. Otherwise, spell them out. For example:
    Each of the 15 procedures, 9 administrative and 6 operating, needed revision.
    Nine instruments, five safety-related and four non-safety-related, need calibrating.
11. Spell out ordinal numbers if they are single words. Write them as numerals if they are not: first, second, third, but 24th, 95th, 100th.
12. Use numerals for fractions: 1/2, 1/4.

3.9.6 Formulas and Calculations

Requiring a user to perform calculations should be avoided as much as possible. As with tolerances using ±, calculations require the user to function on the interpretive level of comprehension rather than the literal level. Use the following guidelines:

1. Eliminate calculations by providing a table of values or a graph.
2. Where calculations cannot be avoided, show the formula, including the units of the terms in the formula. Define all the terms in the formula. Provide space for notations. See the example below.

$$T = \frac{DS \times (A + B)}{A} = \frac{DS__ \times (A__ + B__)}{A__} = \frac{__}{__} = ____ \text{ inch-pounds}$$

where T = Torque required on nut (inch-pounds)
DS = Dial setting or wrench click point
A = Effective torque wrench length (inches)
B = Adaptor effective length (inches)

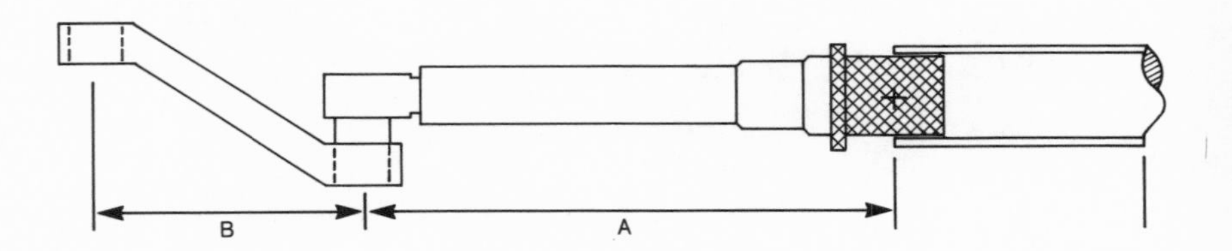

3.10 PROCEDURE GRAPHICS

Procedure graphics are nontext materials that support a procedure, such as figures, tables, data sheets, and checklists. You have identified preliminary graphics in the planning stage. In the drafting stage, you take these preliminary ideas and obtain or develop complete graphics.

This section describes criteria and techniques for graphics in procedures. Generally, procedure writers do not take full advantage of the added dimension of readability and usability that a drawing, diagram, or graph can bring to a procedure. They may not have the time, funds, or support personnel to have graphics developed. However, a diagram showing the location of components, for example, can save a lot of words and possible confusion, so even a neatly hand-lettered diagram is preferable to none.

3.10.1 Criteria

Here are some general criteria. Graphics must be:

- **Appropriate for the intended use**. Graphics can enhance the usability of a procedure, but writers must be careful to ensure that the selected art is actually helpful. Graphics that are unnecessary or too complex may hinder performance.
- **Legible even after reduction (if any) and reproduction**. In procedures on plant systems and equipment, it is logical to use the drawings in vendor manuals or engineering drawings because they will be accurate. However, such drawings may be unsuitable in quality or too large in size to remain legible after reduction and photocopying.
- **Consistent with the procedure text**. This criterion applies to all types of graphics. Component labeling on figures and engineering units on graphs and tables should match those terms and units used in the procedure itself. Forms and data sheets should be designed to follow the text sequence.

- **Completely labeled and identified**. "Attachment 1" is not a very descriptive title for a figure or table. All attachments should have titles. Graphics within the text should be identified by title or by description within the procedure step.
- **Referenced in order in the procedure text**. When graphics (and any other material) are formatted as attachments, Attachment 1 should be the first attachment referenced by the text, Attachment 2 the second, and so on. If your procedure violates this rule, simply reorder the attachments. Once an attachment has been referenced, it may then be referenced at any time and in any order with the other attachments.

3.10.2 Sources of Graphics

When you have identified the need for graphics, you have to obtain the graphics or create them. In this section, we'll cover possible sources of graphics.

1. Determine whether your organization has a graphic arts department. Consult this department for assistance in locating existing drawings or creating new ones. Some departments have a file of drawings already created or used in other documents. You may be able to locate what you need or get ideas on appropriate graphics to include in your procedure.
2. Use the line drawings and diagrams in existing documents as a source of graphics. For example, the following types of documents may be useful sources for technical procedures:
   — Manufacturers' instruction manuals
   — Manufacturers' technical bulletins
   — Architectural drawings and other design documents
   — Electrical diagrams
   — Piping and instrument drawings
   — Similar procedures from other organizations

When reproducing drawings directly from manufacturers' manuals and other existing documents, be sure the copy is legible. The reduction usually required may make the type unreadable.

3. Convert photographs to line drawings by tracing.
4. When new line drawings must be created:
   — Photograph the equipment or the task sequence.
   — Select appropriate view(s) for the drawing.
   — Determine the details you need in the drawing.
   — Trace the photograph to create a line drawing or give a detailed description to a graphic artist to develop a line drawing.
5. When a simple diagram is required, make a rough sketch and label it as desired. Redraw the sketch neatly and paste on typed labels, or give to a graphic artist for drawing and labeling.

3.10.3 Types of Graphics

The term "graphics" encompasses all types of nontext materials supporting a procedure. The four general types are figures, tables, data sheets, and checklists.

Figures. The figures category includes all types of drawings and illustrations, such as the following:

- **Flowcharts**. Many procedure writers attach the flowchart developed in the planning stage to the procedure as a supporting graphic. Such a flowchart summarizes a complex task or process to give the user an overview. The flowchart symbols should correspond to procedure steps exactly, and be numbered with the procedure step numbers. If you developed such a flowchart, ensure that it uses appropriate symbols as follows:

▭ Action step (contains an action verb or task title)

◇ Decision point (contains a question requiring a yes or no answer)

Document (indicates a document is created or completed at this point; contains the document name)

- **Graphs**. A graph represents pictorially the relationship between two variables as these variables increase or decrease. It is useful for presenting a trend, either standard or ideal. A user may also plot a trend with obtained values, generally for comparison with the standard or ideal curve. An example of the graph commonly referenced in industry is a pressure-temperature curve, which indicates how pressure increases with temperature.
- **Illustrations**. An illustration presents in whole or in part the system, equipment, or component with which the procedure is concerned. Illustrations are useful in any procedure to indicate an item's location, for example, a pushbutton on a panel or the packing around a valve. Procedures dealing with equipment maintenance usually require illustrations to show, for example, special tools, how parts fit together in a larger assembly, or the internals of a piece of equipment. Types of illustrations include:
  - **Sketch**. A sketch is a drawing of the subject as seen by the procedure user. It may be two- or three-dimensional, depending on the resources available to the writer and the amount of detail needed by the user. A simple sketch can often be executed by the writer rather than a professional artist.
  - **Exploded View**. An exploded view separates a larger assembly into component parts. It shows the order in which they fit together.
  - **Cutaway**. In a cutaway, the drawing shows the internal parts of a component, as if the component were cut apart and opened to expose the inside. The parts are not separated, but are all in place. Equipment manufacturers use cutaways in their manuals. If you use

such an illustration, consider whether the amount of detail presented is needed for your application. If you use both a cutaway and an exploded view, you will provide the user with a more complete picture of the component.

— **Schematic**. A schematic uses lines and simple symbols to diagram the layout of a system. Schematics are used to illustrate electrical circuits, piping layouts, and relay and other instrument logic. A schematic is relatively easy to draw, and it gives the user "the big picture" of the system with which he/she is working.

— **Sample Forms**. A sample form that is being described in the procedure should be presented as a figure. The user will not use this sample to complete the task, but will obtain a blank form. The sample form should be reduced slightly and boxed. Some companies have an overlay with the word "SAMPLE" that is placed diagonally across the figure. This technique eliminates possible user confusion as to whether he/she should use the copy of the form presented in the procedure. A procedure giving instructions on completing a form may also reference form sections or items by number, and then these numbers are shown on the form to help the user locate the section/item being discussed. Similar to the sample form is the sample document page. For example, a sample procedure cover page is shown as Figure 3-10 in this chapter.

Tables. A table differs from a figure in that it contains only words and numbers, and no line drawings. It presents material in horizontal and vertical columns in which items relate to each other horizontally and vertically. Tables can generally be classified in two categories: tables that present information, and those that present information but are also intended to be filled in by the user. Most tables in the latter category are incorporated in data sheets, but small tables requiring completion are often placed immediately after a step.

Data Sheets. A data sheet, also called a data record, is used to record numerical values or qualitative results determined in a procedure. It may act as a record that the procedure has been completed. Figures and tables may be included on a data sheet.

Checklists. A checklist is used to document that certain steps in a procedure have been performed or to remind a user of steps necessary to complete a task. A checklist may be completed while the procedure is being performed, or it may be completed after task completion as verification that checklist items have been covered. Avoid having a checklist that virtually repeats all the procedure steps. If this repetition is necessary, consider deleting the steps in the instructional section and simply referring the user to the checklist to perform the procedure.

3.10.4 Graphic Techniques to Enhance Figures

Use the following guidelines to ensure the legibility of your graphics:

For all figures

1. As mentioned earlier, exercise caution in reproducing illustrations directly from manufacturers' manuals and other existing documents.
2. Plan a figure so that its final size will be within standard page margins *and* legible.
   - The type size on the original should be large enough that reduction will not make the type unreadable. As a guideline, 12-pitch type is 10 points in height (capital letters). If a figure labeled with 12-pitch type were reduced 50%, the type size would be 5 points. This is the generally accepted lower limit for readable type size.
   - The figure should be laid out so that it is proportional to the 8-1/2″ x 11″ dimensions of the procedure page. Therefore, when reduced, it will still proportionately "fit" the image area without extremely unbalanced margins (white space).

3. The typeface used for labels and callouts should be plain, bold type if possible, but typewriter type or even neat block lettering will still be legible to the user. Use the resources available to you.
4. Reduce oversize figures and ***then*** insert them on procedure pages containing the page number, identification information, and figure number and title in ***full-size type***. Thus, only the figure will appear reduced, not the page identification information. Labeling on the figure may need to be applied after reduction if the reduction makes the type too small.
5. Use foldouts (11″ x 17″ sheets) for oversize illustrations that could be illegible if reduced to 8-1/2″ x 11″. Fold an 11″ x 17″ sheet as follows:
   - Fold the entire sheet in half to the left.

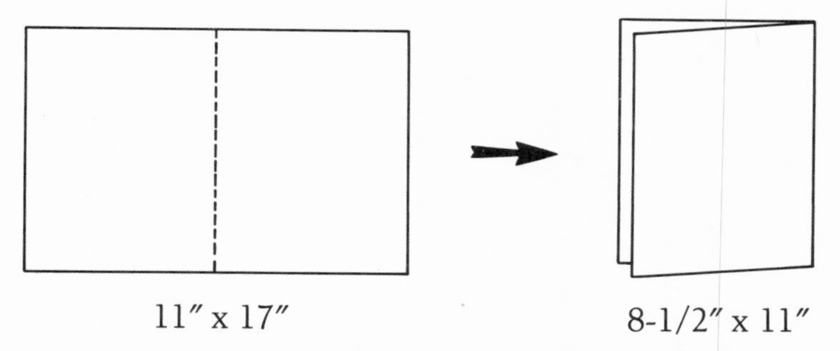

   - Fold one-half of the top fold back to the right:

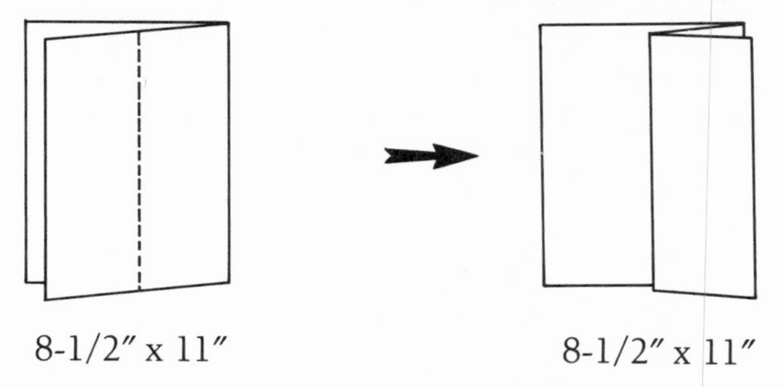

   - Bind the resulting 8-1/2″ x 11″ sheet into the procedure. The foldout may be pulled out to the right to be read.

6. Use foldouts (11″ x 16″ sheets) for an illustration that must be constantly referenced as a task is performed. See Figure 3-14.
   - Arrange the graphic within a 7-1/2″ frame.
   - Have the foldout graphic printed on an oversize, 11″ x 16″ sheet with an 8-1/2″ blank apron.
   - Back the foldout with a blank page.

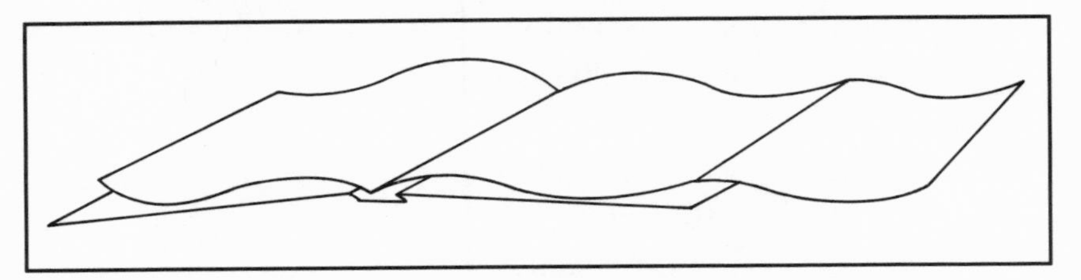

Figure 3-14. Foldout Graphic

7. Ensure that the figure has clear, unbroken black lines that will withstand multiple generations of photocopying.

For illustrations:

1. Avoid shading on illustrations because it does not add technical information. It also reproduces poorly.
2. Keep the illustration simple so that it only represents the needed information. Omit detailed components and parts not directly related to the task.
3. When using labels to identify parts of an illustration, ensure that:
   - Lines from the label to the part clearly indicate the part by touching it.
   - Lines are uniform in thickness, short, and as straight as possible.
   - Lines do not cross.
   - Arrowheads are added.

4. When using numbered callouts to label details in the illustration, ensure that:
   - Numbered callouts are placed in a recognizable order on the illustration.
   - The numbered callout is given in the procedure text immediately after the item is mentioned.
   - No more than 20 numbered callouts per page are used.
   - A key or legend on the figure itself defines each callout number used.

For graphs

1. Ensure that the scale of the graph is consistent with the accuracy the user needs. Thus, the user avoids the need for extensive approximation or interpolation.
2. The background grid (if any) on the graph is clearly reproducible.
3. The grid lines on the graph are distinctly lighter in weight than the axes and the data being presented (the curve). See Figure 3-15.

3.10.5 Table Design

A table may follow a procedure step, or it may be an attachment to a procedure. Wherever a table is placed, it should be referenced in a procedure step with instructions on its use or an explanation of its purpose. Use the following guidelines:

1. If a table is small and relates to a specific step, place it immediately after the step. This type of table does not necessarily need to be titled, but the step should explain its purpose.
2. If a table is to be an attachment, give it a title, which will also serve as the attachment title.
3. Give each column of the table a heading. If every entry in that column is data in the same engineering units, include the units for the data in parentheses in the

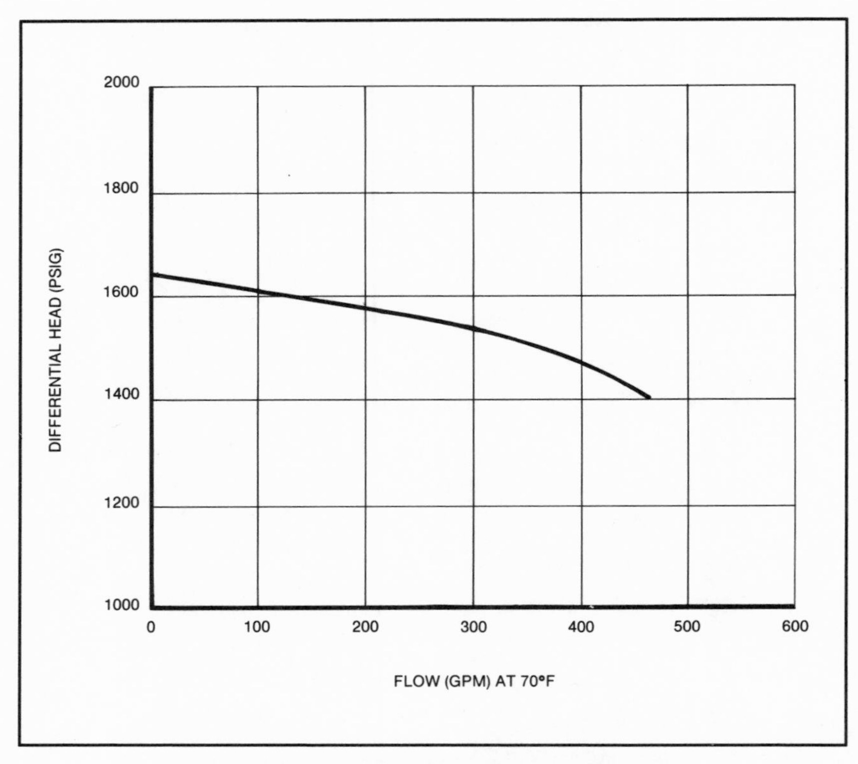

Figure 3-15. Sample Graph

heading; do not repeat the units all the way down the column.

4. If the user is to enter data in the columns, provide adequate space.
5. Use the same type style and size as the procedure text.
6. Place horizontal lines above and below the column headings and at the bottom of the table. Place horizontal lines between each entry when needed for clarity.
7. Place vertical lines between columns unless there is sufficient white space for clarity.

Figure 3-16 is an example of a table.

BOLT DIAMETER (INCHES)	THREAD (PER INCH)	TORQUE (FT-LB)
¼	20	3-3.6
⅜	16	10-12
½	13	27-33
¾	10	95-105
1	8	225-275
1¼	7	450-550
1½	6	790-970
1¾	5	1240-1510
2	4½	1870-2290

Figure 3-16. Sample Table

3.10.6 Data Sheet Design

Data sheets are primarily used to record results of various technical procedures. Give information on the use of data sheets in the procedure steps, on the data sheets, or both. The following types of information may be needed (either in the procedure or on the data sheet):

- For test and calibration procedures:
  - **Equipment Information**. Nomenclature and specifications for the equipment on which the task is performed
  - **Test Equipment Information**. Nomenclature and specification data for the test equipment to be used
  - **Input**. The test conditions required, including tolerances
  - **Output or Required Reading**. Acceptable or desired equipment response, including tolerances
  - **"As Found" or Actual Output**. Space to record the actual equipment response to test conditions

  - **"As Left" or Final Output**. Space to record the equipment response to test conditions following adjustment or repair
- For other procedures, such as maintenance:
  - **Equipment Information**. Nomenclature and specifications for the equipment on which the task is performed
  - **"As Found" Data**. Space for recording actual data obtained
  - **Acceptance Criteria**. Acceptance criteria with tolerances
  - **Spare Parts**. Space for recording any spare or replacement parts used
- For all types of procedures:
  - **Signoff and Date**. Signature (or initials) of the person performing the activity and date of performance
  - **Approval or Verification Signoff and Date**. If required for the activity, space for the signature (or initials) of a verifier or approver of the activity or restoration of equipment after the activity
  - **Signoff and Date**. Signature (or initials) of the person performing the activity and date of performance.

Use the following guidance in designing data sheets:

1. Develop and use a standard format for data sheets for similar types of activities.
2. Ensure that the data sheet has the same procedure identification information as the other pages in the procedure.
3. Give sufficient equipment information to identify it for the user, for example, name, manufacturer name, or model number.

4. For test procedures, give sufficient test equipment information, and provide spaces for the test equipment number and the calibration due date.
5. Avoid putting procedure steps on the data sheet ***instead of*** in the procedure. It is acceptable to repeat certain critical steps and cautions on the data sheet, but be careful, because overuse of this practice may unnecessarily clutter and lengthen data sheets.
6. Always provide acceptance criteria as a range or as a nominal value followed by a tolerance range.
7. Provide adequate space for:
   - Recording data
   - Making calculations
   - Entering any required signoff such as that of the individual performing the work, an inspector, independent verifier, or supervisor
8. Provide a complete reference to the data sheet in the procedure step. For example, state: "Record on Data Sheet 1, Part A" rather than "Record on Data Sheet."
9. Consider giving the corresponding procedure step number next to the data entry point for that step.
10. Arrange data sheets on separate pages and position them at the end of the procedure so that they can be detached easily.
11. Ensure that data sheets are well laid out and not confusing to use. Do not try to put too much on one data sheet. Data sheets should be filled out sequentially with the procedure steps. If the user has to jump from Part C, back to Part A, then down to Part D, your data sheet is not well laid out.

3.10.7 Forms Design

Designing a form is similar to designing a data sheet. In fact, you could consider a data sheet a special type of form. Forms are treated separately here because they are primarily used for nontechnical, administrative purposes, such as keeping a log or requesting a service.

Once you have decided a form is needed for a certain purpose, make a list of the specific items you need to include on the form. This statement may seem obvious, but many times a form calls for too much information that is irrelevant to the user, or it does ***not*** cover everything needed to accomplish its purpose. As you design the form, check off items you have listed.

Consider the following guidelines:

1. Develop and use a standard format for similar types of forms. For example, all types of log sheets should have the same layout, making it easier on word processing personnel ***and*** the user.
2. Provide proper identification information on the form, as required by your company's policy. Identification information includes the form number, revision date, title, and any other items your company may require.
3. Provide adequate space for recording information, and be sure it is clear what goes in each space.
4. Do not try to put too much on one form. A crowded form is daunting to the user. Keep it as simple as you can.
5. If you have too much on one form, consider making a two-sided form or two separate forms altogether.
6. Organize the information into numbered sections with titles, if possible. Then these section numbers can be used in the procedure to help you identify the part of the form for which you are giving instructions.
7. Use bold type, underlining, and full capital letters as methods of emphasis to distinguish items on the form.
8. If your form contains an area that the user is ***not*** supposed to complete, keep it near the bottom of the form, and be sure it is clearly marked.

9. Be sure the instructions on the form are not too cryptic so that they are clear in meaning.
10. Avoid using your department jargon if the form is to be used by outside groups. For example, be careful of "computer-ese" in designing a form that other people will use to request computer services.
11. Try out the form on a potential user to uncover problem areas you may have overlooked.

3.10.8 Typical Graphics Formats

As mentioned earlier in this chapter, graphics are generally formatted as separate attachments or integrated with the procedure text.

Graphics as Attachments. Use the following format guidelines:

1. Number or letter all attachments in sequence. You may also have separate sequences for categories such as figures, tables, and data sheets.
2. Ensure that each attachment contains only one graphic. The title of the attachment should also be the title of the graphic.
3. Arrange attachments in order by number or letter according to how they are used in the procedure; that is, the order of their first mention in the procedure is the order for the attachments.
4. Avoid attaching reference figures or tables that are neither specifically required by nor mentioned in the procedure.

Graphics Integrated with Text. Use the following format guidelines:

1. When graphics are integrated with text, number or letter them in separate series (Figure 1, 2, 3; Table 1, 2, 3). Give each figure or table a title. However, a small figure or table relating to a single step does not require a number and title. (Attachment numbering will be a third, separate series.)

2. Place the graphic immediately after the step that calls it out. If space does not permit this placement, then place the graphic at the top of the very next page, not allowing any following procedure steps to come between the callout step and the graphic. Some pages may need to be shorter or longer to accomplish the best graphic placement.

Avoiding Unacceptable Graphics. Avoid using any of the following for procedure graphics because of reproducibility problems:

- Photographs
- Colored artwork
- Drawings containing illegible lettering or type.

3.11 DRAFTING STAGE: THE FINAL PRODUCT

At the close of your drafting stage, you should have a complete procedure draft that is ready for word processing or typing. If you have graphics in your procedure, you may have already submitted rough sketches for graphic artists to convert to finished line drawings. If you are using integrated graphics, you need to supply the figure or a vertical measurement of the space needed to word processing personnel so that the appropriate space can be left for the graphics.

This procedure draft should be:

- Technically accurate
- Correctly formatted
- Readable, clear, and concise
- Easy to use
- Consistent in format and writing style
- Flexible to accommodate varying task conditions

Your procedure draft is ready for the review stage when it has been word processed or typed. The next chapter discusses procedure review.

4

Review Stage

The review stage of the procedure development process is often overlooked or reduced to a proofreading of the typed draft. Another reason for the lack of an adequate review effort is that many writers, due to procrastination, simply run out of time. While proofing the typed draft is important, it is only one part of the review process.

While some review and revision occur naturally during the drafting stage, the review stage of the writing process requires an objective analysis of the draft to ensure that:

- The procedure is organized correctly by tasks and steps within each task.
- The action steps and related information such as cautions and notes are written correctly.
- All sections of the procedure contain the appropriate type of information.
- The attachments correlate with the information in the body of the procedure and are designed and referenced correctly.
- All standards for mechanics of style have been met.

As you can see from the above list, the procedure writer has a great deal of work to do during the review stage. "Objective" is the key word or concept to remember for this stage of the writing process. Many writers review their work subjectively. It is quite natural to want to keep the words and effort you have put into developing the draft. However, a good writer uses several techniques to separate the creative drafting stage from the objective review stage. Following the Chapter Objectives below, we will look at these general review techniques.

4.1 CHAPTER OBJECTIVES

At the conclusion of this chapter, you should be able to:

- 4.1 State three general review techniques.
- 4.2 Define the two basic tasks of the review stage, verification and validation.
- 4.3 Name the levels of review required.
- 4.4 Apply the Complexity Index to a procedure.
- 4.5 Discuss three consistency checks that must be made.
- 4.6 Name four aspects of a typed document that must be checked during proofreading.
- 4.7 List the two overall criteria for verification.
- 4.8 List the steps in a formal verification process.
- 4.9 List the two overall criteria for validation.
- 4.10 List the steps in a validation process.
- 4.11 Describe each validation method.
- 4.12 List the advantages and disadvantages of each validation method.
- 4.13 Give an example of each of the following types of questions: open, closed, probing, and leading/loaded.
- 4.14 State two types of nonverbal communication that would occur in a validation debriefing.

4.2 GENERAL REVIEW TECHNIQUES

Objective review techniques include setting aside time between the drafting and review stage; involving others in the review process; and using your planning product, a checklist, or other objective criteria to evaluate the draft. The advantages of these techniques are discussed below.

4.2.1 Involving Others in the Review Process

Involving others in the review process, concurrent with your review, allows you the opportunity to get constructive feedback before the procedure enters the formal review process. Those persons who can give you the most helpful informal feedback are a peer and a representative from the user group.

An informal review system established with peers and users has proved to be a successful review method. This system requires several rules to be established to make it successful:

- First, the system must be reciprocal; that is, all or several members of the peer group must agree to review each other's work.
- Second, the level and type of review expected and the objective must be clearly stated. For example, consider the following ways to request a review:
  - "Look this over and let me know what you think."
  - "Would you review the instructional steps by Friday, and tell me whether the sequence is the way you actually do it?"
  - "Does this make sense to you technically? Don't worry about the typos at this point. I need your comments by tomorrow."

  Each of the above requests would result in a different type of review and feedback. The first request is too general; the reviewer does not have enough specific direction on what to do. The second and third requests will result in more constructive, specific comments that you can use to improve the procedure.
- Third, enough time must be allowed for the review.
- Fourth, the method of feedback must be clearly stated.

This system has several advantages for both the writer and the reviewers. The writer receives valuable information about the adequacy of the procedure before a supervisor evaluates the draft. In other words, the writer has an opportunity to receive feedback and improve the draft in a nonthreatening situation (feedback that will not be used in such activities as performance appraisal). In addition, the peers and users learn from the review process. Peers may identify some writing techniques, both positive and negative, that they may want to use in their own writing. User representatives will appreciate the opportunity to participate in the review of a procedure before the procedure is approved for use and they are responsible for performing the procedure as written.

A peer serves as an excellent reviewer because usually he/she has a similar background of training and also writes procedures. The peer, however, does not have the emotional and intellectual investment in the procedure that you have and therefore can be more objective. The user representative reviews the procedure from an experiential point of view. He/she reads and evaluates the procedure from the perspective of "Will the procedure work as written?" and "Are there enough details?" Thus, from both groups the procedure writer receives information that will be useful in revising the draft.

4.2.2 Time

Have you ever written a product and then immediately tried to review/revise the document but found that even though you may have noticed changes you wanted to make, you did not know how to make the changes? If your answer is yes, you are not alone. Most writers, even the most successful and renowned professionals, experience this problem. The answer is often simply a matter of time.

Why do you need time between the drafting stage and the review stage? You need time to make the transition from being the creator of the message to the critic of the message. Trying to review the draft objectively immediately after it is created reduces your chance of being an objective evaluator of the message because the ideas developed are still fresh in your mind. For whatever period of time it took to develop the draft, you have been thinking about the content of the messages developed in the procedure. Every writer needs a "cooling off" period from the drafting stage to the review stage to develop the mind set of being a critic of the message.

4.2.3 Structured Reading: Comparing the Draft to Objective Criteria

To sustain objectivity in your own review of the draft, you should apply the process of "structured reading." Structured reading simply means objectively reading your procedure by comparing it to one or more objective criteria. In essence, you are auditing the draft against these criteria, which include:

- Your expanded outline
- A review checklist, either an existing one used by your department or organization, or one you have devised yourself. A checklist should include technical criteria that deal with the content and human factors criteria that deal with the format and writing style.

Comparing the draft to the outline will reveal any differences in the scope and sequence of the procedure. Your draft will not necessarily be exactly the same, but if changes were made, you should evaluate why you made the changes. The more complete your outline is, the more effective is this technique.

Comparing the draft to a checklist is effective because you may not have remembered all the technical and human factors criteria that you should have kept in mind while drafting the procedure. The checklist will jog your memory.

4.3 TWO REVIEW TASKS

We can divide the review stage into two tasks:

- First, an objective review of the procedure's (1) technical content and (2) written correctness in terms of your corporate format and human factors drafting principles as described in your writer's guide. This task is essentially a "desktop" task. This task may be termed "Verification."

- Second, a review of the "paper" procedure versus the actual task as it is performed at the worksite. To be done thoroughly this task involves a walkthrough at the site with a typical user. This task may be termed "Validation."

The following sections discuss these tasks in detail.

4.4 VERIFICATION: THE WRITER'S PERSPECTIVE

Verification can be viewed from two perspectives: the writer's and the independent reviewer's. From the writer's perspective, verification is an objective but *informal* process. For example, the writer involves another reviewer informally, and is soliciting opinions that he/she can ultimately reject. However, verification can also be performed *formally* by an independent reviewer, as part of your company's review and approval process for procedures. A formal verification is a slightly different approach, which is described in the next section. However, ideally, the formal reviewer should consider all the aspects of verification discussed here while reviewing a procedure.

After drafting a document, a writer often just rereads the words and looks for typographical errors. Such a review is highly subjective because the writer is simply reading his/her own words. Moreover, many writers read linearly; that is, they read from page 1 to the end. Because so many technical and human factors criteria must be evaluated, this process is the least efficient method of reviewing a procedure. The suggestions in this section seek to make your review objective. These techniques may apply to your own review or to anyone you have review your procedure.

4.4.1 Levels of Review

You should review your draft procedure on several levels, beginning with the general level and moving to the specific:

- **Organization**. The first level is the general organization of the procedure. Ensure that all the appropriate sections of the procedure are developed, and check for appropriate breakdown of major tasks.

- **Sequence**. This level focuses on the sequence of steps in the instructional section. Review the steps to determine whether the technical sequence of the tasks, steps, and substeps is correct.
- **Step**. This level focuses on the individual steps. Review each step for technical accuracy and appropriate sentence structure and vocabulary.
- **Mechanics**. At this final level, proof the typed draft for mechanics such as spelling, spacing, margins, and page breaks.

4.4.2 The Complexity Index

The Complexity Index is an objective technique you can use to rapidly assess your procedure steps for excessive complexity (Brune & Weinstein, 1980).

- Count the number of steps in the procedure. If the procedure is long, use two or three pages.
- Count the action verbs in the steps. For example, "*Weigh* ten parts individually and *average* the results to obtain the part unit weight."
- Divide the number of action verbs by the number of steps.
- If the resulting index is greater than 1.5, look at the individual steps to see whether any should be broken down. If a step contains two or three *related* actions, it is acceptable. Related actions are those that are done in close sequence or lead to a certain result, such as "*Depress* and *hold* the pushbutton."

4.4.3 Consistency Review

We mentioned earlier that you should avoid a linear review. If you properly check for consistency, it is impossible to perform only a linear review. Before you can check for consistency, you must first remove the staple or the paper clip holding the procedure together. Then you can more easily check for consistency on several levels, specifically:

- **Attachments**. Each time the text refers to an attachment, immediately check the attachment to ensure the reference is correct.
- **One Section and Another**. When the text of the procedure mentions another section of the same procedure, immediately check the referenced section to ensure the referencing instruction is correct.
- **The Procedure and Others It References**. If you have referenced another procedure or document, check your notes or the referenced document itself to ensure the referencing instruction is correct.

If you are reviewing a procedure that you have revised (rather than prepared from scratch), this consistency check is just as important. Procedures that have gone through several revisions are especially prone to consistency problems. Often, a revision consists of inserting a few steps in an existing procedure, and more often than not these additions are not verified for consistency with the rest of the procedure. The inserted steps may be inconsistent in structure, writing style, or vocabulary. In addition, the inserted steps change the step numbering scheme, so that cross-referencing from other steps may need to be changed.

Another problem we have seen with procedures that have been revised numerous times is the nonexistent figure, table, or note. A step will refer the user to Figure 4. Unfortunately, Figure 4 was dropped three revisions ago, and none of the revisers or reviewers checked the entire procedure for possible cross references. A careful review will avoid this problem.

A last point on consistency: the time it takes to review for consistency seems to increase exponentially with the length of the procedure because there are more pages to review and the chance of missing something increases. Here are two techniques that may help you:

- For consistency in spelling and terminology, keep a "style sheet" on words and phrases that may be spelled or hyphenated different ways. For example, by the time you reach page 70, you may not remember whether the phrase "high-pressure seals" or "high pressure seals" was used earlier in the procedure. If you keep a style sheet on these "gray areas," it was save you a great deal of searching.
- Make use of word processing capabilities to perform automatic global searches to track down terms that may be spelled inconsistently or to find the illusive reference to Figure 4 that you need to change to Figure 3. Also use the capability to copy material exactly. For example, you are tasked with writing or revising a procedure that contains four virtually identical sections on four models of the same component. Have word processing personnel electronically copy the first section three times. Then, you only need to edit these copies to tailor them to the different models. The advantages of this method are threefold: (1) you save time in drafting, (2) you save time in reviewing because you essentially need to check only one section thoroughly, and (3) you can deliver to the user a procedure that is consistently worded and therefore easier to perform.

4.4.4 Proofreading for Mechanics

Most procedure writers do not have access to an editorial or proofreading staff who can proofread their procedures for them. Therefore, you may very likely be responsible for proofreading the typed procedure.

Use the following techniques for thorough proofreading:

- Always proofread the newly typed copy against the original. Proofreading without the original may cause you to miss omitted steps or paragraphs, because sometimes a procedure may seem to make sense even with the omissions.

- Proofread numerical values carefully against the original.
- Proofread all titles and section headings carefully. Inexperienced proofreaders tend to skip these items and go right to the body of the text, and then are embarrassed to have missed an obvious "typo" that the reader/user will immediately notice.
- Proofread words and phrases in full capital letters carefully. It is easy to miss typographical errors in such words.

Proofreading is not just checking for typographical errors. In addition, you will need to check for appropriate type style and size, line spacing, page margins, and page breaks.

Type Style and Size. For procedure text, use the type style that is standard across all procedures in your department or company. Examples of type styles commonly used are:

LETTER GOTHIC	ABCDEFGHIJKLMNOPQRSTUVWXYZ abcdefghijklmnopqrstuvwxyz !@#$%¢&*()_+,.'"?/., 1234567890
PRESTIGE ELITE	ABCDEFGHIJKLMNOPQRSTUVWXYZ abcdefghijklmnopqrstuvwxyz !@#$%¢&*()_+,.'"?/., 1234567890
COURIER	ABCDEFGHIJKLMNOPQRSTUVWXYZ abcdefghijklmmopqrstuvwxyz !@#$%¢&*()_+,.'"?/., 1234567890

The type size for procedure text should generally be 12 pitch, that is, 12 characters to the inch. The previous examples are 12 pitch.

Line Spacing. Proper line spacing enhances readability. For example, if a procedure were entirely single-spaced or entirely double-spaced, a user would have difficulty distinguishing among steps, sections, cautions, and notes.

The most readable procedures use a combination of single and double spacing as follows:

- Single spacing within the following:
  - A paragraph
  - A step or substep
  - A caution or note
- Double spacing as follows:
  - Between paragraphs
  - Between steps and substeps
  - Before and after section headings
  - Before and after cautions and notes

The following line spacing for lists is recommended:

- Lists of short items (no more than one line each) should be single spaced.
- Lists should have a double space between items when at least one item is two or three lines long.

Page Margins. Sufficient page margins on all four edges ensure that material is not accidentally cut off in photocopying. You should take care to properly size (and reduce if necessary) graphs and other illustrations. The following page margins are recommended:

- All four edges: at least 1″ margin between text and page edge
- If a header such as a procedure number is in the top corner, at least 1/2″ margin above it
- If a page number is at the bottom of the page, at least 1/2″ margin below it

Page Breaks. Page breaks, that is, where one ends and another begins, can detract from readability or even cause user errors if they are not checked properly. Although a word processing system automatically breaks pages, you, the procedure writer (and therefore proofer), should check each break against the following criteria:

1. Avoid ending a page with a heading. The heading must be followed by at least one step or two lines of text.
2. For paragraphs, avoid a single, "widow" line at the bottom or the top of a page. Make sure there are at least two lines of text on either side of a page break.
3. Avoid breaking a two- or three-line step between pages.
4. Avoid ending a page with a colon.
5. Avoid separating a caution from its step, and never split the text of the caution between pages.
6. Avoid separating a note from its step by a page break.
7. If a series of critical steps must be done rapidly, keep them all on one page.

4.4.5 The Verification Checklist

You will recall that at the beginning of this chapter we discussed using an objective criterion such as a checklist to guide the review process. You should develop such a checklist for verification, and another for validation (discussed later in Section 4.6.4 of this chapter).

Use the following guidelines to develop a Verification Checklist:

1. Develop a checklist that is as generic as possible, but you will probably find that a checklist is needed for each procedure category because of different technical and format criteria.
2. Consider developing two verification checklists, one for technical criteria and one for human factors criteria. One organization used this approach because different personnel were verifying the two areas.
3. Organize the checklist in one of the following ways:
   - By section of the procedure

- By level of criteria, that is:
  - General or global issues such as procedure identification and pagination
  - Issues related to individual sections (such as criteria for prerequisites)
  - Criteria for individual step construction
  - Criteria for graphics and attachments

  In either case, group technical questions together and human factors questions together; do not mix them in a sequence.

4. Supply the following columns for response:
   - Yes
   - No
   - N/A
   - Comment No.

   At the end of the checklist, give space to list and discuss comments by number.

This checklist will serve for both the writer's review and the independent reviewer. The independent reviewer's perspective is discussed in the next section.

4.5 VERIFICATION: THE INDEPENDENT REVIEWER'S PERSPECTIVE

The general definition of verification as the first review task, a "desktop" activity, still holds for the independent or formal review. However, verification in the formal sense requires that another person, not the writer, evaluate the technical source material to ensure that the technical information is correct, complete, and up to date. It also requires that this verifier review the procedure against human factors criteria and company standards for procedure format, such as the procedure writer's guide. The verification process is guided by the Verification Checklist we just described in Section 4.4.5.

4.5.1 Verification Principles

As with the writer's perspective of verification, the formal verification process is concerned with two major principles or criteria, technical accuracy and written correctness.

Technical Accuracy. The independent verifier must ensure that the procedure is technically accurate. Specific aspects of technical accuracy include:

- The technical source material should be accurate and up to date.
- Tolerances should be expressed as ranges to reduce the possibility of error.
- Equipment names, equipment numbers, parts, and units of measure should match the technical sources.
- Verifications, signoffs, and approvals should be included as needed or required by company policy.

Written Correctness. The independent verifier must ensure that the procedure is written correctly according to the company writer's guide, standard formats, and basic, human-factors-based tenets of information presentation. Specific aspects of written correctness are:

- The appropriate format should be consistently used to improve the procedure's readability.
- The level of detail should be complete enough for the least qualified user to perform the task.
- User decisions must be made in a logical order, and instructions must be provided for all possible decision outcomes.
- Figures, tables, and data sheets should be useful and well designed to reduce the chance of error.
- Adequate room for calculations should be provided where calculations are required.
- Referencing and branching should be minimal. If used, references should be complete, appropriate, and correct.

- Sufficient identification information must be presented to identify every page of a procedure.

4.5.2 Verification Process

The verification process consists of four steps.

1. **Assemble Documentation**. The procedure writer assembles for the reviewer all the technical source documents used to develop the procedure, as well as documents related to writing a procedure. The reviewer also receives a Verification Checklist and blank discrepancy forms (if used).
2. **Verify the Procedure**. Using the Verification Checklist and the source documents, the reviewer compares the draft procedure to the criteria presented in the checklist and the procedure's technical information to the source documents.
3. **Document the Verification**. The reviewer notes any discrepancy between the checklist criteria and the procedure. The reviewer may document these discrepancies on the procedure itself and in the Comments section of the checklist. Some organizations also use discrepancy forms as additional documentation. Figures 4-1, 4-2, and 4-3 are sample forms. Figure 4-1 is used to record each discrepancy and has a space for resolution. Figure 4-2 is a summary form that lists all the discrepancies for one procedure. Figure 4-3 is a form used to document completion of the verification and satisfactory resolution of the discrepancies.
4. **Resolve Verification Comments**. The procedure writer reviews the reviewer's comments, including any discrepancy forms and the checklist, and revises the draft procedure as appropriate.

DISCREPANCY FORM

Procedure No. ____________

Step No. ________________

Problem Type

____ Procedure Problem

____ Equipment Problem

____ Communication Problem

____ Other ______________

Description Discrepancy

Suggested Resolution

Action Taken:

Action Taken by: ______________________ ______________________

Signature Date

Figure 4-1. Sample Discrepancy Form

DISCREPANCY SUMMARY

Procedure No. ______________________ Title ______________________

Discrepancy No.	Step No.	Description	Resolution	Date Resolved

Form Completed by ______________________ Date ______________________

Figure 4-2. Sample Discrepancy Summary Form

PROCEDURE VERIFICATION COMPLETION

Procedure Title ______________________________

Procedure Number ______________ Revision ______________

1. Resolution accomplished for all applicable discrepancy forms. ______________

2. Verification process is complete. ______________

Verifier Signature ______________ Date ______________

Writer Signature ______________ Date ______________

Approved by ______________ Date ______________

Figure 4-3. Sample Verification Completion Form

4.5.3 Summary of Verification from the Two Perspectives

We have discussed verification from two perspectives, the writer's and the independent reviewer's. Each has a different process to follow in verifying a procedure. The writer is more concerned with written correctness, having already checked technical accuracy in the planning stage by using the most up-to-date sources. The independent verifier, however, focuses equally on technical accuracy and written correctness, guided by the Verification Checklist. For verification in its most complete sense, the verifier checks all the sources the writer has used to ensure the procedure reflects them precisely and without error. The verifier is also concerned with written correctness, but if the writer has performed his/her verification thoroughly, this review will not require nearly the time the writer has spent in review.

Now, the next task is validation.

4.6 VALIDATION

As we described at the beginning of this chapter, validation is a comparison of the procedure with the actual task and environment. The purpose of a validation is to ensure that the procedure will work in practice. A technically accurate procedure will not work if the user cannot follow it or if he/she tends to misinterpret the steps because they are confusing.

Validation, the principles, methods, and skills needed, will be discussed here from only one perspective: the validator. This does not mean the writer does not, cannot, or should not validate his/her own procedure. On the contrary, the process described here is no different for an independent validator or the writer. The process is the same, but the thoroughness of the process can be adjusted for the writer according to the time or resources available. You will recall in planning that we suggested a walkthrough to determine any environmental considerations affecting the task performance. If you performed this walkthrough in planning, the validation should hold no surprises for you.

As you, the writer, read through the following sections, consider *yourself* as the validator. For each procedure, you will need to determine the method and the level of effort needed for validation.

4.6.1 Types of Errors Identified during Validation

Regardless of the method used to validate a procedure, you will notice performance errors. Usually, these errors can be classified as user errors and procedure errors. Identifying the type of errors made will help you revise the procedure or identify nonprocedure problems that should be addressed, such as improving training.

Generally, user errors mean that information was available to the user in the procedure but it was not used. User errors are:

- Noncompliance—For example, a procedure was available but not used or followed.
- Omission—A procedure was used but steps were not performed.
- Incorrect Action—A procedure was used but an error was committed in the performance of a step.
- Commission—A user selects the wrong control or mis-positions a control.
- Error of Timing—A user performs a step too early, performs a step too late, or performs a step stated in the procedure but not in the proper sequence.

Procedure-related errors are:

- Technically Inaccurate Procedure—Instructions in a procedure were incorrect.
- Incomplete Level of Detail—Instructions in a procedure were incomplete. The procedure did not contain the level of detail needed by the user.
- Outdated Procedure—The procedure did not reflect changes in equipment or limits.

4.6.2 Validation Principles

Although some aspects of the validation principles discussed below sound similar to verification, the two processes are not repetitive. Normally, verification is a "desktop" exercise; validation is concerned with performance.

Validation is concerned with two major principles or criteria, user compatibility and plant compatibility. (We will use the term "plant" here to refer to the worksite, whether it is a plant, an office, or a field location.)

User Compatibility. The validator must ensure that the procedure is compatible with the user. Specific aspects of user compatibility include:

- The level of detail should be sufficient to allow the user to use his/her knowledge to perform the procedure. Look for signs of unbalanced detail. Too much detail might cause resistance to use; insufficient detail could result in hesitation or errors.
- The procedure should include all relevant information (no omissions) and only relevant information (no distractions). Look for signs of procedure voids; for example, a user must use equipment responses or information not specified in the procedure. Also look for procedure irrelevancies; for example, the performance time is excessive because the user must read through marginally relevant information.
- Procedures should be structured and written so that the user comprehends the information. Look for rereading of steps and hesitation in performance.
- Format relates to different types of information presentation such as text (words), tables, and graphs. Consider what format is best suited to a given situation. For example, is text the best technique to describe choices and contingencies, or should flowcharts be used?

- Referencing and branching instructions should be clear to the user. Look for user difficulties in following these instructions.
- Procedural descriptions for team application should not be in conflict with staffing considerations. Look for difficulties with individual responsibilities (does each user seem to know what to do and when to do it?) and coordination (do the users know whether and how their responsibilities affect and are affected by other team member actions?).
- Many problems in using a procedure at the job site can be traced to the physical characteristics of the procedure. Look for potential user problems such as the need for excessive flipping back and forth between pages of the procedure. Other symptoms are not as easily traced to physical aspects; for example, no means of placekeeping extends the performance time.

Plant Compatibility. The validator must ensure that the procedure is also compatible with the environment in which it is used. There is some overlap between plant and user compatibility because the two (plant and user) interact. This interaction ultimately determines the procedure's usability. Specific aspects of plant compatibility are:

- The physical characteristics of a procedure must be suitable for the environment. For example, a potential user problem is work space. Does the user have a flat work space to lay down a procedure that is printed double sided?
- Some procedure steps need to specify location for equipment items infrequently used, difficult to locate, or not labeled. Look for user difficulties in locating equipment.
- Conditions described in the procedure should match the actual condition of the plant or equipment. Observe how

the equipment responds to a user action. Errors will occur when a procedure leads the user to expect that an action will result in "A," but the equipment responds with "B" and "C."

- User performance should be consistent with the physical aspects of the equipment. Look for problems with timing. (Can the user physically move to all involved locations in a reasonable time and without impeding movement of co-workers?)
- The procedure should take into account unusual communication needs. For example, can a user understand a verbal instruction about the procedure when wearing ear protectors?

4.6.3 Validation Process

The basic steps in validation are similar to those in verification, with one additional step, debriefing, which occurs after the procedure is validated and before documentation is produced.

1. **Prepare for Validation**. This step is equivalent to the "Assemble Documentation" step in verification, although more preparations must be made. The validator must arrange for the chosen validation method (described in Section 4.6.4 below). For example, if a walkthrough is the validation method, the validator must schedule a user to walk through the procedure and must obtain clearance (if needed) to walk through the procedure in the plant.
2. **Validate the Procedure**. This step is the actual performance of the chosen validation method.
3. **Debrief Participants**. This step is needed for all validation methods because they all involve others besides the validator. Later in this chapter, we will discuss communication skills useful for conducting a debriefing.
4. **Document the Validation**. Similar to verification, the validator documents discrepancies between the proce-

dure and the validation criteria. Discrepancy forms similar to those used in verification, a Validation Checklist (see Section 4.6.5), and a markup of the procedure itself are useful documentation.

5. **Resolve Discrepancies**. As in verification, the procedure writer addresses and resolves the discrepancies found in the validation, revising the procedure as appropriate.

4.6.4 Validation Methods

A procedure can be validated by several different methods. Each has its advantages and disadvantages.

For all of these methods except the talkthrough, consider photographing the task sequence. The photographs will help resolve possible conflicting comments made by the validation team members during the debriefing.

Walkthrough in the Plant. In the presence of a validator, a user performs and explains the procedure, step by step, using either nonoperational equipment or on-line equipment. In the latter case the user cannot actually operate the equipment.

Advantages:

- Faster than the actual performance method
- Can be combined with training
- Relatively inexpensive
- Allows time for interruptions, questions, answers, and user reactions
- Allows validator to observe user reactions
- Allows validation of most or all steps that do not require hardware responses
- Will not damage equipment

Disadvantage:

- Does not allow validation of hardware responses to user actions

Walkthrough in a Laboratory or Mockup (such as a mockup of a control room). In the presence of a validator, a user performs and explains the procedure, step by step, on laboratory equipment or a mockup of equipment.

Advantages:

- Faster than the actual performance method
- Can be combined with training
- Relatively inexpensive using an existing laboratory or mockup
- Allows time for interruptions, questions, answers, and user reactions
- Allows validator to observe user reactions
- Allows validation of steps that do not require plant responses
- Will not damage plant equipment

Disadvantages:

- Does not allow validation of hardware responses to user actions
- Not an accurate validation if the mockup does not exactly match the actual plant

Talkthrough or Tabletop. A user or group of users interprets and evaluates procedure information, answers questions, and "talks through" the steps in the presence of the validator. There is no access to the equipment or a mockup.

Advantages:

- Convenient
- Relatively inexpensive
- Can be repeated as often as necessary
- Can be performed anywhere

Disadvantages:

- Cannot validate equipment nomenclature

- Cannot use equipment responses to test the user's decisions
- Cannot check how procedures are used in the field

Actual Performance. A validator observes a user performing the sequence of steps as described in the *approved* procedure with plant equipment.

Advantages:

- Most exacting method. Reflects the "real world."
- Can observe equipment response.

Disadvantages:

- Could damage equipment if procedures are incorrect
- Time consuming
- Must use approved procedure

4.6.5 The Validation Checklist

The Validation Checklist is a document essential to the validation process. As with the Verification Checklist, it lends objectivity and structure to the review. Generally, however, the two checklists are used differently. The Verification Checklist is completed concurrently with the verifier's review. The Validation Checklist is completed after the walkthrough or talkthrough, based on notes taken during these events.

Use the following guidelines to develop a Validation Checklist:

1. Develop a checklist that is as generic as possible, addressing the validation principles discussed above in Section 4.6.2. You should find it easier to have a generic checklist for several disciplines than was the case with verification.
2. Organize the checklist according to the two validation principles, user compatibility and plant compatibility, and develop specific questions related to these principles.
3. Include space to indicate the validation method used.

4. Use the same numbering scheme and format as for the Verification Checklist for consistency.
5. Supply the same response columns as for the Verification Checklist (Section 4.4.5).

Review the checklist to prepare for validation, and complete it after the validation. During debriefing, consider having the user(s) complete the checklist or give their responses to the checklist items. Then, the validator should finalize the checklist for post-validation documentation.

4.6.6 Communication Skills for Validation

A successful debriefing is a critical element of the validation process. The debriefing allows the validator an opportunity to gain additional information and clarify perceptions developed during the preparation and implementation phases of the validation process. A key element the validator must keep in mind is that the user's cooperation in the validation process will determine whether the objective of the validation can be met. Cooperation can best be obtained if a professional, businesslike atmosphere can be established and maintained.

Atmosphere refers to the psychological climate needed to maintain a channel of communication. Factors that influence this climate are the:

- User's understanding of the validation process
- Validator's nonverbal behavior
- Physical design of the debriefing situation

Through the debriefing session, the validator uses a variety of communication skills to gain the information needed to complete a successful validation effort. The communication skills needed in a debriefing situation are questioning skills and active listening skills.

Questioning Skills. The type of question asked during the debriefing influences the climate of the debriefing situation and the amount and type of information received. The four basic types of questions are:

- Open
- Closed
- Probing
- Leading and loaded

The validator should plan a few key questions, usually the open type, after the validation exercise.

- **Open Questions**. Open questions ask for general information and allow the user to structure the response. Open questions such as "What do you think were the strong points of the procedure?" allow the user to give his/her opinion of the usability of the procedure. This approach helps establish the cooperative atmosphere needed to have an effective validation.

  Answers to open questions provide the validator with information that can be used to formulate other types of questions. In addition, the user does not feel that the validator is passing judgment on his/her performance.

  Disadvantages of open questions are:

  — They increase the time needed to conduct the debriefing.

  — Note taking is more difficult.

  — The user may feel the validator is not sure what he/she is looking for.

  Rule of Thumb: Use open questions to start each debriefing session. These questions usually begin with "What do you think of . . .?"

- **Closed Questions**. Closed questions are designed to limit the response available to the user. Usually a closed question can be answered with a single word or phrase. "Was the procedure usable?" is a closed question. This question, if answered yes, leaves the validator struggling to continue the discussion. If the validator disagrees with the user's perception, he/she will have to ask a series of closed questions just to keep the discussion going.

The advantages of closed questions are:

— Many questions can be asked in a short time.

— Note taking is easier.

— The validator controls the debriefing.

— They help focus on specific points of information.

The disadvantages of closed questions are:

— They limit the amount of information given.

— If they are not used properly, the user can be made to feel pressured, as if he/she is on trial.

— They can rapidly deteriorate a cooperative climate.

Rule of Thumb: Use closed questions only when seeking a specific item of information. Try not to ask more than three closed questions in succession.

- **Probing Questions**. Probing questions are used to clarify information received or to seek additional information, usually based on a response to an open question. For example:

  "Could you give me an example of what you mean by insufficient instructions?"

  Probing questions are useful because they focus the response on the information you need to know. For example:

  "Could you explain what would happen if the equipment were not warmed up?

  Probing questions can be used to clarify apparent inconsistencies in user responses, such as:

  "You stated the procedure needs better graphics. Would you identify where the graphics are needed and which types of graphics would be best?"

Probing questions help the validator control the debriefing and keep the topic from wandering.

Rule of Thumb: Use probing questions to indicate to the user that you are listening and comprehending the messages being received.

- **Leading and Loaded Questions**. For the most part, leading and loaded questions are detrimental to a debriefing. These questions require the respondent to agree with a position held by the validator. A user will resent being asked to agree with the point of view of the validator if he/she does not hold the same view. For example, "Don't you agree the procedure needs a lot of work?" is a leading question.

Table 4-1 lists purposes for asking questions and indicates which type(s) of question is appropriate.

Table 4-1. Summary of Question Types and Purposes

	Question Types		
Purpose	**Open**	**Closed**	**Probing**
1. To get information without creating defensiveness	X		
2. To allow the user to express personal opinions	X		
3. To gather more specific points of information		X	X
4. To eliminate misunderstanding of the type of answer solicited		X	X
5. To guide the discussion toward a specific problem		X	X
6. To help determine what the user sees as being important	X		X
7. To help prevent presenting your beliefs prematurely	X		
8. To obtain more information			X
9. To clarify points that have been made			X

Active Listening Skills. After asking a question, the validator evaluates the information and attitude of the user, and reacts in a manner to foster a positive atmosphere. The validator's reactions, both verbal and nonverbal, indicate active listening to the user. Failure to indicate active listening will limit the amount of information offered by the user and negatively influence the atmosphere for communication. Some users may not want to be involved with the validation effort, but a user may be more likely to cooperate if the validator uses active listening skills.

Active listening provides the user with feedback. This feedback is provided through paraphrasing, summarizing, and nonverbal responses.

- Paraphrasing. Paraphrasing is using your words to indicate understanding of a user's response. This technique fosters a positive atmosphere because it shows users you are paying attention to their remarks.

  Paraphrasing should be used when the validator feels an important point of information needs to be understood by both parties. For example, "If I understand you correctly, if you were to perform the steps as written, the task could not be performed correctly?"

  Notice that the paraphrase can serve as a lead to a line of questioning. If the user responds "Correct" to the paraphrase, it serves as a closed question. But, if the validator's perception/comprehension was not correct, the paraphrase serves as an open or probing question requiring the user to provide more information.

- **Summarizing**. This technique can be used at the end of each area of discussion, as well as at the end of the debriefing. Summarizing differs from paraphrasing because *all* the key points are covered in summarizing. For example, "Let's go over all the steps that were out of a logical sequence."

  This technique is useful when a great deal of information has been discussed, especially in response to an open question. Summarizing can also be used when the validator feels the user's responses are vague. Rather than keep asking a series of questions to gain clarification, the validator can summarize the information given to that point to indicate where more information is needed to be useful. For example, "So far you've given me information about the two tasks, but I'm still not clear about your opinion of the usefulness of the System Description section."

- **Nonverbal Responses**. Nonverbal responses are both given and received from the user. A person communicates between 50 and 80 percent of his/her comprehension or feelings about the information through nonverbal behavior.

  The validator uses nonverbal behavior such as the following to indicate his/her level of comprehension to the user:

  — Facial expressions
    - Interest/disinterest
    - Belief/disbelief

  — Body language
    - Boredom
    - Aggression

  — Physical arrangement of the debriefing setting

  A validator also receives nonverbal responses from the user that indicate the user's comprehension and attitude about the information or situation. The validator must be aware of these signals and develop the appropriate strategy to maintain a positive atmosphere. For example, if it is determined through the user's nonverbal behavior that he/she does not understand a question, the validator can rephrase the question.

4.6.7 Detailed Validation Procedures

As we said earlier, validation involves a choice of methods. The method chosen will affect the procedure followed. Appendix B contains suggested procedures for each validation method discussed above.

4.7 SUMMARY

We have discussed reviewing a procedure as two tasks, verification and validation. The actual process of procedure review and approval will vary among organizations, but you, as the writer, should always review your procedure before it enters any kind of a formal review process. It bears repeating that you should approach your procedure ***objectively***, and that you should perform your own verification and validation before a formal review. Use the techniques described in this chapter, and then review the Verification and Validation Checklists to ensure you have met all the criteria.

Now that you are aware of how your procedure should be reviewed (by yourself or an independent reviewer), you can apply many of these techniques to planning the procedure. Most helpful are involving the user and performing a walkthrough. If you take the time to do these in planning, you will reap the benefits in the review stage.

References

American Nuclear Society, *Administrative Controls and Quality Assurance for the Operational Phase of Nuclear Power Plants*. ANSI/ANS-3.2-1982. New York: American National Standards Institute, 1982.

Blaiwes, A. S. "Formats for Presenting Procedural Instructions." *Journal of Applied Psychology* 59 (1974): 683-686.

Brune, R. L., and M. Weinstein, Sandia National Laboratories. *Checklist for Evaluating Emergency Procedures Used in Nuclear Power Plants*. NUREG/CR2005. Prepared for the U.S. Nuclear Regulatory Commission. Washington, D.C.: Government Printing Office, 1981.

———. *Development of a Checklist for Emergency Operating Procedures Used in Nuclear Power Plants*. NUREG/CR-1970. Prepared for the U.S. Nuclear Regulatory Commission. Washington, D.C.: Government Printing Office, 1981.

———. *Development of a Checklist for Evaluating Maintenance, Test and Calibration Procedures Used in Nuclear Power Plants*. NUREG/CR-1368. Prepared for the U.S. Nuclear Regulatory Commission. Washington, D.C.: Government Printing Office, 1980.

———. *Procedures Evaluation Checklist for Maintenance, Test and Calibration Procedures*. NUREG/CR-1369. Prepared for the U.S. Nuclear Regulatory Commission. Washington, D.C.: Government Printing Office, 1980.

Carver, R. P., American Institutes for Research. *Improving Reading Comprehension: Measuring Readability*. AD-780-448. Prepared for the Office of Naval Research. Washington, D.C.: Government Printing Office, 1974.

Coleman, E. B. "Improving Comprehensibility by Shortening Sentences." *Journal of Applied Psychology* 46 (1962): 131-134.

Foster, J. J. "Legibility Research - The Ergonomics of Print." *Icographic* 6 (1973): 20-24.

Fuchs, F., J. Engelschall, and G. Imlay, Xyzyx Information Corporation. *Evaluation of Emergency Operating Procedures for Nuclear Power Plants*. NUREG/CR-1875. Prepared for the U.S. Nuclear Regulatory Commission. Washington, D.C.: Government Printing Office, 1981.

———. *Human Engineering Guidelines for Use in Preparing Emergency Operating Procedures for Nuclear Power Plants*. NUREG/CR-1999. Prepared for the U.S. Nuclear Regulatory Commission. Washington, D.C.: Government Printing Office, 1981.

Gates, A. I. "What Do We Know about Optimum Lengths of Lines in Reading?" *Journal of Educational Research* 23 (1931): 1-7.

Heuertz, S., and J. Herrin. "Validation of Existing Nuclear Station Instrument and Electronics Procedures to Reduce Human Error: One Utility's Perspective." *IEEE Transactions on Energy Conversion* EC-1 (December 1986): 12-17.

Institute of Nuclear Power Operations. *Writing Guideline for Maintenance, Test, and Calibration Procedures*. INPO 85-026 (Preliminary). Atlanta: Institute of Nuclear Power Operations, 1985.

Institute of Nuclear Power Operations, Emergency Operating Procedure Implementation Assistance (EOPIA) Group. ***Emergency Operating Procedures Validation Guideline***. INPO 83-006. Atlanta: Institute of Nuclear Power Operations, 1983.

———. ***Emergency Operating Procedures Verification Guideline***. INPO 83-004. Atlanta: Institute of Nuclear Power Operations, 1983.

———. ***Emergency Operating Procedures Writing Guideline***. INPO 82-017. Atlanta: Institute of Nuclear Power Operations, 1982.

Jay, F., Editor in Chief. ***IEEE Standard Dictionary of Electrical and Electronics Terms***, 2d ed. IEEE Standard 100-1977. New York: Institute of Electrical and Electronics Engineers, Inc., 1977.

Kammann, R. "The Comprehensibility of Printed Instructions and the Flow Chart Alternative." ***Human Factors*** 17 (1975): 183-191.

Klare, G. R. ***A Manual for Readable Writing***. REM Co., 1975.

Miller, E. E. ***Designing Printed Instructional Materials: Content and Format***. HumRRO RP-WD(TX)-75-4. Alexandria, Va.: Human Resources Research Organization, 1975.

Parker, S. P., Editor in Chief. ***McGraw-Hill Dictionary of Scientific and Technical Terms***, 3d ed. New York: McGraw-Hill, 1984.

Peterson, L. V., and W. Schramm. "How Accurately Are Different Kinds of Graphs Read?" ***Audio Visual Communication Review*** 2 (1955): 178-199.

Redish, J. C. ***Beyond Readability: How to Write and Design Understandable Life Insurance Policies***. American Council of Life Insurance, 1985.

Savolainen, A., R. H. Feldman, W. E. Oliu, and M. H. Singh. ***Technical Writing Style Guide***. NUREG-0650. Prepared for the U.S. Nuclear Regulatory Commission. Washington, D.C.: Government Printing Office, 1979.

Seminara, J. L., W. R. Gonzalez, and S. O. Parsons, Lockheed Missiles & Space Co., Inc. ***Human Factors Review of Nuclear Power Plant Control Room Design***. EPRI-NP-309. Palo Alto, Calif.: Electric Power Research Institute, 1977.

Strunk, W., Jr., and E. B. White. ***The Elements of Style***, 3d ed. New York: Macmillan, 1978.

Taylor, W. L. "Cloze Procedure: A New Tool for Measuring Readability." ***Journalism Quarterly*** 30 (Fall 1953): 415-433.

U.S. Nuclear Regulatory Commission, Division of Human Factors Safety of the Office of Nuclear Reactor Regulation. ***Guidelines for the Preparation of Emergency Operating Procedures***. NUREG-0899. Washington, D.C.: Government Printing Office, 1982.

Words into Type, 3d ed. Englewood Cliffs, N.J.: Prentice-Hall, 1974.

Wright, P., and F. Reid. "Written Information: Some Alternatives to Prose for Expressing the Outcomes of Complex Contingencies." ***Journal of Applied Psychology*** 57 (1973): 160-166.

Appendix A

Word Usage*

accuracy, precision

Accuracy is the agreement between the true value and the result obtained by measurement.

Precision is the agreement among repeated measurements of the same quantity.

activate, actuate

Both words mean "to make active," although *actuate* is usually applied only to mechanical processes.

Example: The relay *actuates* the trip hammer.

Activate usually is more appropriate for a procedure action verb, that is, when a person is "to make active." *Activate* also has a wide range of applications to chemical processes, for example, to make something photosensitive or more adsorptive.

---

* This appendix is adapted from A. Savolainen, et al., *Technical Writing Style Guide*, NUREG-0650, prepared for the U.S. Nuclear Regulatory Commission (Washington, D. C.: Government Printing Office, 1979), 59-67.

affect, effect

Affect is a verb that means to influence.

Example: The Supervisor's decision affected all employees.

Effect can function either as a verb that means to bring about or to cause, or as a noun that means a result.

Examples: The Director *effected* several changes in the department that had a good *effect* on morale.

Avoid using *effect* as a verb. A less pompous-sounding substitute, like *made*, is preferable.

alternate, alternative

To *alternate* (verb) is to occur in successive turns.

An *alternative* (noun) is a choice among mutually exclusive objectives or courses of action.

analyze, determine, identify

To *analyze* is to separate into parts to *determine* the nature of the whole.

To *determine* is to ascertain definitely, as after an investigation or calculation.

To *identify* is to name a thing or to ascertain its origin, nature, or characteristics.

and/or

Avoid this overworked expression. State your meaning exactly.

Change: X and/or Y

To: X or Y or both

apt, liable, likely

Apt means exactly suitable, to the point, appropriate.

Liable means "legally subject to" or "responsible for" and connotes legal responsibility.

Likely means probable.

assure, ensure, insure

Assure, ***ensure***, and ***insure*** all mean "to make secure or certain."

Assure refers to persons, and it alone has the sense of setting a person's mind at rest.

Example: The fire department ***assured*** the public that there was no risk of exposure.

Both ***ensure*** and ***insure*** mean "to make secure from harm." However, only ***insure*** has the connotation of guaranteeing life or property against risk and should be reserved for use only in this sense.

Examples: A systematic approach will help ***ensure*** a properly written procedure.

The corporation needs to ***insure*** itself against large liability claims.

balance, remainder

Balance means both "a state of equilibrium" and "the amount remaining in a bank account after balancing deposits and withdrawals."

Remainder always means "what is left over." Use ***remainder*** to mean "what is left over" outside of bookkeeping contexts.

because, since

Because is the strongest and most specific connective used to state a causal relationship.

Example: The procedure was retyped ***because*** it required many revisions.

Since is a weak substitute for ***because*** when expressing cause. It is, however, the appropriate connective when the emphasis is on circumstances or conditions rather than on cause and effect.

Example: ***Since*** all the inspections proved the plant to be operable, the proposed startup schedule was approved.

compose, comprise, consist, include

Compose means "to create" or "to make up the whole" of something. Parts *compose* (make up) a whole.

Examples: Cement, aggregate, and water (the parts) *compose* concrete (the whole).

Concrete is *composed* of cement, aggregate, and water.

Comprise means "to embrace" or "to include." The whole *comprises* the parts. Use the active voice, "comprises." The passive voice, "is comprised of," is incorrect.

Example: A botanical garden (the whole) *comprises* trees, flowers, and other plant life (the parts).

Consist means that *all* parts making up a whole are listed, but *include* does not.

Examples: Concrete *consists* of cement, aggregate, and water.

Concrete *includes* cement and aggregate.

conclude, decide, determine

To *conclude* is to *decide* or judge after careful consideration.

To *decide* is to make up one's mind, as after doubt or debate.

To *determine* is to establish or ascertain definitely.

continual, continuous

Continual means intermittent or repeated at intervals.

Continuous means without interruption in time, or of unbroken extent in space.

data

Data may be used as a singular or plural noun in current American usage. However, in very formal technical writing, as for a scientific journal, the strict use of *data* as a plural noun is more appropriate. The Latin singular, *datum*, is used as a surveying term.

definite, definitive

Definite means unmistakable, precise, or having certain limits.

Definitive refers to something complete or authoritative.

due to, because of

Due to in the sense of "caused by" is acceptable in phrases following a form of the verb "to be."

Example: His fall was ***due to*** carelessness.

Due to is not acceptable when it follows other verbs and is used to mean "because of."

Change: He fell ***due to*** carelessness.
To: He fell ***because of*** carelessness.

etc.

A series introduced by the words "for example," "includes," or "such as" should not be followed by ***etc.*** because the phrases, taken together, are redundant. (*Etc.*, when used in text, is followed by a comma except when it ends a sentence.)

Avoid using ***etc.*** in procedures. State what you mean exactly. Using ***etc.*** introduces vagueness into the sentence.

factor

Factor has a precise mathematical meaning. Do not use it unnecessarily even in mathematical contexts, however. The expression "to increase by a factor of 3" means simply to triple—use triple.

farther, further

Farther refers to distance.

Further indicates additional degree, time, or quantity.

Example: As you go ***farther*** away, your ability to hear is ***further*** decreased.

fewer, less

Fewer refers to units or individuals.

Less refers to mass or bulk.

Example: With the use of *less* powder, *fewer* particles result.

foreword, forward, preface

Forward is very often confused with the word *foreword*. Even though *forward* describes a position of something located toward the front, it is not the correct word to describe introductory material in a book or report. The term *foreword* usually applies to a statement about a book or report written by someone other than the author. A *preface* is usually a statement by the author that describes the purpose, background, or scope of a book or report. However, the terms *foreword* and *preface* are often used interchangeably.

i.e., e.g.

i.e. means "that is."

e.g. means "for example."

Use the English equivalents to avoid misuse, overuse, pompousness, and misinterpretation.

impact, impacted

Impact used as a noun means the actual striking of one body against another, or the impression of one thing on another. It is often misused to mean *effect*.

Change: That revision will have an *impact* on all department policies.

To: That revision will have an *effect* on all department policies.

Impact used as a verb means to cause to strike forcefully. It is often misused to mean *affect*.

Change: That revision will *impact* many other procedures.

To: That revision will *affect* many other procedures.

imply, infer

Imply indicates by association or consequence rather than by direct statement.

Example: The neatness of the report *implies* that the typist is proud of his work.

Infer derives a conclusion from facts or premises.

Example: We *infer* that the data are correct.

interpolate, extrapolate

You *interpolate* (meaning estimate) between two known values.

You *extrapolate* (meaning infer or predict) from the values of a known series.

mutual, common

Mutual refers to two persons or things, and means reciprocally exchanged.

Common means shared by all.

on the order of

Do not use *on the order of* to mean about or approximately. If you mean "within an order of magnitude," say so.

only

Place *only* immediately before the word or phrase it modifies. Note the difference in meaning caused by the word's location in the following sentences:

Examples: He was the *only* engineer.
He was *only* the engineer.

opposed to, compared to

Do not use *opposed to* unless you mean in literal opposition; use *compared to* instead.

Examples: Force a is *opposed to* force b, and is stronger.
Force a *compared to* force b is several times greater.

order of magnitude

Use this phrase to express measurements in powers of 10 only, not to mean "approximately."

Example: The earth's mass is about 10^{24} kg; that of the sun, 10^{30} kg. Their masses differ by about six ***orders of magnitude***.

parameter

A ***parameter*** is an arbitrary constant or an independent variable through functions of which other functions may be expressed.

Examples: The ***parameters*** for the first test were 6 to 12 V.

Four ***parameters***, three in space and one in time, are needed to specify an event.

practical, practicable

Practical means useful in actual practice.

Practicable means capable of being put into practice.

presently, currently

Presently means in a short time, soon, directly. It does not mean now or at this time. To denote now, use ***currently***.

principal, principle

As a noun, ***principal*** means head or chief; as an adjective, it means highest or best.

Principle means basic truth, law, or assumption.

prior, before

Prior is an adjective meaning earlier in time or order.

Before as an adverb means in advance; as a preposition it means in front of or preceding.

Example: He was hired according to ***prior*** agreement, an agreement reached ***before*** his arrival.

procure

Procure is an overworked word. Buy, obtain, or purchase is preferable.

proved, proven

Proved is preferred as the past participle of the verb to prove.

Example: He has proved his point.

Proven is better used as an adjective.

Example: He has a proven record of achievement.

providing, provided, if

Do not use ***providing*** in the place of ***provided*** or ***if***.

Example: *Providing* jobs is difficult now, but will be easier ***provided (if)*** next year's budget is adequate.

shut down, shutdown

Shut down is a verb form (action).

Examples: ***Shut down*** the pump (imperative).

DO NOT perform maintenance until the turbine has been completely ***shut down*** (passive voice).

Shutdown is a noun or adjective (condition).

Examples: The plant is in a ***shutdown*** condition.

The procedures for plant startup and ***shutdown*** are being revised.

start up, startup

Start up is the verb form (action).

Example: The corporation has received approval to ***start up*** the plant.

Startup is a noun or adjective (condition).

Example: The corporation has received approval for plant ***startup***.

that, which

That is appropriate to restrictive (defining) clauses that are not set off by commas.

Example: The specifications *that* are in dispute (only those in dispute) have been referred to the engineer.

Which is appropriate to nonrestrictive (nondefining) clauses that are always set off by commas.

Example: The specifications, *which* are not acceptable (none of them are acceptable), have been returned to the vendor.

via

Via is Latin for "by way of." Restrict its use to routing instructions.

Example: The package was sent to New York *via* Baltimore.

Do not use *via* to mean *through* or *as the result of* outside of such contexts.

viz

Use *namely* or *that is* instead of *viz* when introducing examples, lists, or items.

whether, if

Whether implies a condition of doubt.

Example: He was not sure *whether* security was breached.

If implies no alternative.

Example: *If* it does not rain, we will move the equipment.

while, although, whereas

The noun *while*, when used in adverbial phrases, indicates a period of time (during, or at the same time as). When used as a conjunction, *while* means "as long as" in reference to time. ***While*** should not be used in the place of ***although***, ***whereas***, ***and***, or ***but***.

Although (conjunction) means regardless of the fact that or even though.

Whereas (conjunction) means in view of the fact that and is commonly used to indicate a comparison or contradiction.

Appendix B

Validation Procedures

This appendix contains procedures for each validation method:

- Walkthrough
- Walkthrough in Laboratory or Mockup
- Talkthrough
- Observation of Actual Use

VALIDATION PROCESS—WALKTHROUGH

Preparation

1. Read the verified procedure to identify potential problems.
2. Develop preliminary performance and discussion questions.
3. Review training records regarding qualifications needed to perform the procedure.
4. Meet with the user to:
   - Explain the reasons for the walkthrough.
   - Collect appropriate user information.
   - Explain the walkthrough process.
5. Obtain a camera and film.

Implementation

1. Observe the user role play performing the procedure.
2. Take photographs of the task, concentrating on such areas as equipment labeling.
3. Ensure the user moves to all physical locations required by the procedure.
4. Ask performance questions such as "What if?" or "How would you?"
5. Notice environmental conditions that could affect performance.
6. Mark the procedure with your comments and the user's.

Debriefing

1. Ask general (open) questions to get the user's opinion about the procedure's strengths and weaknesses.
2. Ask specific (closed or probing) questions to get answers to your concerns and comments.
3. Note the answers on the procedure or separate sheets.

Documentation

1. Complete post-validation documentation:
   a. Consolidate comments on a clean copy of the procedure.
   b. Identify deviations from the Writer's Guide.
   c. Determine whether resolution is required for deviations.
   d. Complete discrepancy forms for the deviations as required by policy.
   e. Finalize the Validation Checklist.
   f. Revise the procedure.
   g. Process the procedure according to company policy.
2. Retain discrepancy forms and the Validation Checklist as a record of the review.

VALIDATION PROCESS—WALKTHROUGH IN LABORATORY OR MOCKUP

Preparation

1. Read the verified procedure to identify potential problems.
2. Walk through the environment of procedure use.
3. Develop preliminary performance and debriefing questions.
4. Review training records regarding qualifications needed to perform the procedure.
5. Ensure the laboratory or mockup is available and specific to procedure use.
6. Meet with the user to:
   - Explain the reasons for the walkthrough.
   - Collect appropriate user information, including the user's years of experience.
   - Explain the laboratory or mockup process.
7. Obtain a camera and film.

Implementation

1. Have the user read and explain how he/she would use the information not related to equipment, for example, Prerequisites.
2. Have the user perform steps that require actions on equipment.
3. Take photographs of the task, concentrating on such areas as equipment labeling.
4. Have user comment on information in the procedure.
5. Observe performance, noting any user verbal and non-verbal clues to comprehension.
6. Ask questions regarding problem areas and record user responses.
7. Record any discrepancies observed.

Debriefing

1. Ask general (open) questions to get the user's opinion about the procedure's strengths and weaknesses.
2. Ask specific questions regarding your observations.
3. Note the answers on the procedure or separate sheets.
4. Have the user complete the preliminary Validation Checklist.

Documentation

1. Complete post-validation documentation:
   a. Consolidate comments on a clean copy of the procedure.
   b. Identify deviations from the Writer's Guide.
   c. Determine whether resolution is required for deviations.
   d. Complete discrepancy forms for the deviations as required by policy.
   e. Finalize the Validation Checklist.
   f. Revise the procedure.
   g. Process the procedure according to company policy.
2. Retain discrepancy forms and the Validation Checklist as a record of the review.

VALIDATION PROCESS—TALKTHROUGH

Preparation

1. Read the verified procedure to identify potential problems.
2. Walk through the environment of procedure use.
3. Develop preliminary discussion questions and scenarios.
4. Review training records regarding qualifications needed to perform the procedure.
5. Meet with user to:
   - Explain the reasons for the talkthrough.

- Collect appropriate user information, including the user's years of experience.
- Explain the talkthrough process.

Implementation

1. Have the user read through the procedure, explaining what he/she would do with the information.
2. Have the user explain the physical and mental processes needed to perform each step, for example, manipulate dials, calculate.
3. Have the user role play specific steps such as turning back to data sheet, graphics, and references.
4. Ask questions about the problem areas identified in the Preparation phase.
5. Periodically ask questions about steps with a low level of detail to determine the user's in-depth understanding.
6. Record comments and responses on a copy of the procedure or on separate sheets.

Debriefing

1. Ask general (open) questions to get user feedback.
2. Ask specific (closed or probing) questions regarding specific section information (appropriate test equipment, graphics).
3. Ask the user about possible environmental factors that could affect performance.
4. Have the user complete the preliminary Validation Checklist.

Documentation

1. Complete post-validation documentation:
   a. Consolidate comments on a clean copy of the procedure.

b. Identify deviations from the Writer's Guide.
c. Determine whether resolution is required for deviations.
d. Complete discrepancy forms for the deviations as required by policy.
e. Finalize the Validation Checklist.
f. Revise the procedure.
g. Process the procedure according to company policy.

2. Retain discrepancy forms and the Validation Checklist as a record of the review.

VALIDATION PROCESS—OBSERVATION OF ACTUAL USE

Preparation

1. Read the verified procedure to identify potential problem areas.
2. Develop preliminary debriefing questions related to identified problem areas.
3. Review training records regarding the qualifications needed to perform the procedure.
4. Meet with the user to:
   - Explain the reasons for the walkthrough.
   - Collect appropriate user information, including the user's years of experience.
   - Explain the observation process.
5. Obtain a camera and film.

Implementation

1. Conduct an over-the-shoulder observation of procedure use.
2. Take photographs of the task, concentrating on such areas as equipment labeling.
3. Note environmental conditions as to how they affect performance and whether they were considered in the procedure.

4. Identify any discrepancies from procedure instructions.

Debriefing

1. Ask general (open) questions to get the user's opinion of the procedure's strengths and weaknesses.
2. Identify any discrepancies observed and discuss them with the user.
3. Have the user complete the preliminary Validation Checklist.

Documentation

1. Complete post-validation documentation:
   a. Consolidate comments on a clean copy of procedure.
   b. Identify deviations from the Writer's Guide.
   c. Determine whether resolution is required for deviations.
   d. Complete discrepancy forms for the deviations as required by policy.
   e. Finalize the Validation Checklist.
   f. Revise the procedure.
   g. Process the procedure according to company policy.
2. Retain discrepancy forms and the Validation Checklist as a record of the review.

Index